Introduction
TO THE
Italian Rapier

A Step-by-Step Guide to the
Fundamentals of Rapier Combat by

Devon Boorman

Freelance Academy Press
Wheaton, IL 60189
First Edition
©2017 by Devon Boorman

Printed in the United States of America

No part of this book may be reproduced or used in any form or by any means without prior
written permission of the publisher.

Cover and interior design and production: Greg Reimer

Printed in the United States of America by Publishers' Graphics

21 20 19 18 17 16 14 13 12 1 2 3 4 5

ISBN: 978-1-937439-24-8
Library of Congress Control Number: 2017958945

DEDICATION & ACKNOWLEDGEMENTS

Writing a book is no small feat. This, my first, has been a labour of several years. It started as a 600 page magnum opus and then through good advising and revision became the more succinct primer it is today. I have learned a tremendous amount about writing, about my art, and about myself through this process and I am grateful for all the help that I've had along the way.

Thank you to Tom Leoni for his inspiration, access to excellent translations of works on fencing, and for his friendship. Thank you to Greg Mele for helping me make the choice to cut the manuscript down significantly and his encouragement to embark on many other publishing projects. Bonita, my partner in life, cannot avoid mention for her encouragement, support, and editing! And a big thank you to Greg Reimer who has been a true partner in crime for the past several years as my stalwart assistant on both sides of the camera, a brave challenger of my work, and an inspiration for much of how I approached this material.

I must thank my excellent students, and models, who have brought the techniques described to their visual form: Adrian Jones, Matheus Olmedo, Audrey Hui, Aurelia Sedlmair, Greg Reimer, and Clinton Fernandes.

Many others have played a role as editors, reviewers, and supporters, they include: Maestro Puck Curtis, Marco Quarta, Guy Windsor, Gary Spechko, Selman Halabi, Roland Cooper, Dan Read, Andre Kostur, and Bernd Petak. Thank you all for reading this book and giving me such earnest and useful feedback.

It is rare to find good fencing in this world. It is a struggle to realize an art which is both beautiful and terrible in its potential to kill. The beauty of good fencing is a living painting created through years of effort which vanishes within a fraction of a second and observers lucky enough to be present may be the only ones to see the artist's greatest work. To bring it into existence the artist must possess a special blend of athleticism, access to a well-organized system of combat, and dedication to practice and study both physical and mental.

In my own pursuit I spent years training, studying, and finally enduring board examinations to ensure that I was qualified to teach. It was in this skeptical place that I found myself when I first attended the Vancouver International Swordplay Symposium in 2011 and from the salon above the fencing floor I observed the school's fencers below. Their arms were extending cleanly before the lunge and flowing smoothly forward into attacks. Without taking my eyes from the floor I spoke to my colleague, M. Eric Myers, and asked, "Do you see this?" He agreed; something special was happening at the Academie Duello and it continues to this day.

One key to unlocking the fencing of any tradition is access to good teaching. A good teacher with hundreds of hours of experience on the floor sword-in-hand will sharpen the explanations of fine, nuanced, and difficult topics. They learn different methods of presenting information and actions which speak to different kinds of students. To teach fencing is to create artists and realize a new kind of art but the medium, the pieces, are human beings improved by the process of guided training. They in turn manifest their own art in the world like ripples flowing outward from the school affecting lives in ways little and large, simple and profound.

In the years since, I have come to know the students of the Academie better and their teacher, Maestro Devon Boorman. M. Boorman is a world class fencer who rose from the ranks of the Society for Creative Anachronism as one of the bright lights of their rapier tradition both in skill and character. The school he founded is internationally renowned and he has traveled the world to teach, fence, and lecture about the Italian tradition. One of the systems taught in the school is Italian rapier from the early 1600s with some of the jargon and theory gently and lovingly polished for clarity. I find it most closely aligned with Capo Ferro but easily part of the same family as Giganti and Fabris.

What will you find within the pages of this book? Imagine that Capo Ferro was able to write plainly to an audience in English and that he had clarified the ambiguities of his text. That he had further codified the system and provided flowcharts and additional detail of execution, tempo, and distance. Beyond illustrating exemplar martial plays he also provides a strategic structure for the tradition which guides the moment-to-moment tactics.

The result would be something like what you hold in your hand today. On a bookshelf with works by Agrippa, Viggiani, Fabris, Giganti, and Capo Ferro there is room for at least one more work. M. Boorman's new book (and others written by his modern day peers) are this generation's essential contribution to the family of Italian fencing.

I think you will find it of considerable value as you train, struggle, and finally create art within yourself.

July, 21 2017
~R. E. "Puck" Curtis III
Master at Arms,
San Jose Fencing Master's Program

CONTENTS

Chapter One

Good king of cats, nothing but one of your nine lives;
that I mean to make bold withal, and as you shall use me
hereafter, drybeat the rest of the eight. Will you pluck your
sword out of his pitcher by the ears? Make haste, lest mine
be about your ears ere it be out.
—Mercutio to Tybalt, William Shakespeare, *Romeo and Juliet*, 1595

INTRODUCTION TO THE RAPIER

Welcome to the first chapter in your journey in wielding the
Renaissance rapier. In these opening pages you will learn a little of my
history, the history of the rapier, how to approach this book, and the
fundamentals to getting started in your own learning. I recommend
reading the introduction thoroughly to get the most out of these
instructions and to best understand my approach.

I invite you now to turn the page and set off on your journey to learn
one of the most beautiful, efficient and deadly of martial arts.

My Journey and Yours

The rapier is a wonderfully iconic weapon. The favoured sword of the Three Musketeers, Cyrano de Bergerac, and Hamlet. It was the sword dashingly wielded by Errol Flynn and Basil Rathbone in classic movies like *The Sea Hawk* and *Captain Blood*. It was Romeo's tool for vengeance against Tybalt and Paris in Shakespeare's *Romeo and Juliet*. It appears at the side of nobles and soldiers in portraits painted by the great baroque masters Rembrandt and Caravaggio. It resolved affairs of honour for notable figures such as Shakespeare's contemporary, Ben Jonson,[1] and was perhaps the tool responsible for severing Van Gogh's ear.[2]

In the modern world, when many think of the rapier they think of the Olympic fencer dressed in fencing whites and fighting on a long linear track. Olympic fencing, however, has become quite distinct from its ancestor. The weapons used in modern fencing bear little practical connection to their historical counterparts. They are as little as a quarter the weight of a real weapon and exceptionally flexible. The intricacy and strategy of the art is often reduced to the application of a few simple movements performed with herculean strength and speed. The introduction of electronic scoring, initially in 1936[3] also changed the sport significantly as moves designed simply to press the button on the end of the sword became further emphasized over those that could genuinely wound with a sharp blade.

For me the rapier was the weapon from the black and white reruns of Zorro[4] (played by Tyrone Powers) that I watched as I grew up. It was the sword wielded by the Man in Black and Inigo Montoya in *The Princess Bride*. It was a weapon of grace, wit, and daring deed that embodied the dashing qualities of these fictional characters. I was so enamoured with this deadly tool that I used to dance about in the backyard of my childhood home with a foil my parents had found in the attic, making up fencing moves and imagining myself — as young boys do — as one of my favourite heroes.

The specifics for the actual historical rapier are rather hard to pin down. The idea of classifying swords by their design into neat well-titled categories — rapiers, court swords, smallswords, arming swords, sideswords, etc — is a product of Victorian curators eager to categorize their collections and simplify the evolution of weapons into something clean and orderly. Yet even with this desire the qualities that they used to designate one sword as a member of one group versus another are often hard to identify. If you wander through a museum you can see a great many weapons labeled as rapiers, yet they can range from short, heavy, and broad-bladed, to the exceedingly long, thin, and without sharp edges. Written historical sources are not much further help. Nearly all historical texts from the Renaissance, whether fictional, biographical, or instructional, simply refer to the swords within as just that: "swords".[5]

The term *rapier* in modern martial arts usage has come to refer to a particular sword pictured and described in historical fencing manuals that were published primarily in the 1500s and 1600s. The sword I am referring to is primarily a civilian sword that was worn on the city street and wielded in private duels rather than on the battlefield. It had a long and slender blade with a sharp point and the strategies for using it were oriented toward the thrust as the primary method of wounding. Metal plates, sweeping bars and intricate rings on the hilt extended out to protect the hand and shield the body of the wielder, a significant innovation from most earlier swords that simply had a blade, grip, and crossbar.

I had my first opportunity to wield a rapier (or at least a modern facsimile of one) when some friends brought me to a Renaissance festival outside of Seattle, Washington, run by the Society for Creative Anachronism. There I had the chance to watch a re-creation of a rapier tournament and I was immediately enthralled. There was certainly a storybook quality to watching people dressed up in historical clothing, but what grabbed me most was the swordplay itself. It was fast, deft, calculated, intricate—everything I had wanted it to be. I saw that this was a weapon finely tuned for one on one combat. Its length and speed emphasized the concepts of distance and timing, and its subtle mix of caution, control, and commitment fit within a strategic and tactical framework of move, counter-move, invitation and deception that blew me away.

When the fencing stopped, I got to meet one of the fencers who was an instructor in my area and I was suddenly caught up in an impromptu lesson. As soon as I had a sword in my hand, I was hooked. Twenty years later, I continue to be enchanted with this weapon. Though I have studied many different martial arts (both Eastern and Western), I feel that no weapon or discipline has furthered me more as a martial artist than the rapier. To this day, I am still finding new ways to improve and deepen my understanding of the art on a regular basis.

In 2004, I co-founded Academie Duello in Vancouver, BC, with Randy Packer, one of my senior students at the time. Although our full system includes two-handed swords, one-handed cutting swords, pole weapons, unarmed combat, and mounted combat, the rapier is an essential and foundational part of our system.

Many students, both at Academie Duello and other schools, begin with the arming sword or sidesword, weapons used in one hand and based around the arguably more intuitive cut, or the two-handed longsword, the mechanics of which are often seen as being easier to teach and learn. The system for Italian Rapier is more physically demanding than those of these other weapons, and has a much broader and more rigorous theoretical base. Because of its length and point-oriented nature it is a superb teacher of range and timing. It teaches you about lines and angles and control and constraint of the opponent through its strong emphasis on blade position and interaction. Once you have gained proficiency with the rapier, the techniques and principles of the system can be applied to all of the other weapons, giving one a significant advantage in further learning. When you progress to the sidesword and longsword you will already have the most important combat fundamentals in place and can focus on cutting and crossing of lines, body position and the other skills needed to wield these weapons. The rapier is to swordplay what the piano is to the study of music; It is not an easy start, but investment in it will pay long-term dividends both physically and mentally for any practitioner.

My goal with this book is to set out the fundamentals for my approach to Italian Rapier. I think you will find that the system of the rapier I present, though sophisticated, is easy to grasp, elegant and effective. Though duels of honor are no longer a feature in our society, practice of this martial art will help you become a more physically able, confident, and noble person. These are truly the lasting ideals of martial arts training.

History of the Rapier

The rapier is a product of military evolution, social pressure, fashion, and hot blooded conflict. To truly understand its origins we must start with the changing face of warfare in the late 1400s and 1500s. Battles throughout the European Middle Ages had long been the realm of small group conflict. Regional militia with simple weaponry combined with groups of highly trained mercenaries and noble soldiers. The weapons and armor of the wealthy elite included the two-handed sword, polearm, full suits of plate, and horses, used in skirmish oriented engagements with other heavily armored knights. These were highly experienced warriors who had the necessary time, money, and individual training that a noble could afford.

However in the 1400s military conflict was changing. Political and military powers were consolidating, particularly in Northern Italy and Germany. More powerful fortifications were being built and military forces were moving away from smaller militias and mercenary bands to larger, well-funded, standing armies. These larger armies, now in the thousands, instead of the hundreds, were armed with increasingly reliable guns and artillery and employed significantly more advanced formations. Armored cavalry, noble soldiers, and elite mercenaries, were becoming a thing of the past.[6]

Although the place for nobles was diminishing on the battlefield, the pressure for them to show individual prowess at arms remained. Castiglione, in his influential *Book of the Courtier* (1528) writes "The principal and true profession of the courtier ought to be that of arms." He goes on to state that a courtier is expected to be adept with the weapons normally used not only in war, where no great subtlety is needed, but also in the combat that frequents quarrels between gentlemen.[7] Fortunately, an institution had already been well established that embraced and legitimized these gentlemanly conflicts, and gave an outlet for demonstrating military skill: the duel.

Duelling over matters of honor, in Europe, had been well established as part of the judiciary process since at least the 1400s.[8] This form of court sanctioned conflict at arms followed the military fashion of the time and was typically performed in armor with lance and sword. Yet, as fashion changed so did the conventions both of the duel and its weapons. The historian and fencing master Pietro Monte in his 1509 fighting treatise speaks harshly of the increasing number of duels being fought in shirtsleeves instead of armor.[9] His comments tell us both of duelling's chivalric origins and the evolution of its practice in the later Renaissance. These new duels were fought with civilian weapons over civilian causes. Duelling without armor was seen as more equitable. It did not require military equipment or training, so your means were a much lesser factor in your ability to emerge as victor.[10] It also occurred within a much more controlled environment than a battlefield. Though many earlier authors on the art of arms had focused on a broader system of fencing, that could be applied both in duels and in more diverse encounters,[11] a new mode of fencing was emerging that focused purely on the civilian encounter.

"Because of the diabolical modern invention of artillery, all that remains to us of the good ancient ways of military honor is the duel"[12] says Camillo Agrippa in the introduction to his 1556 fencing manual. Agrippa was an engineer, architect, and fencer who lived in Rome. His *Treatise on the Science of Arms* was a revolution in fencing that leveraged a scientific approach while expressing the duel's new sensibilities. It shed old modes of thought in swordplay and paved the way for a new approach to fencing. Although Agrippa's weapon largely resembled the battlefield weapon of his contemporaries, now typically called a sidesword,[13] his system of fencing was the first designed around a more thrusting-centric approach, tuned to the unarmored conflict. This new type of fencing was even more attractive to the noble class. It was more scientific and allowed for nobles to both express and differentiate themselves through a knowledge of geometry and mathematics, while simultaneously showing their prowess in affairs of honor. This was seen as more dangerous, and thus more valorous, because it was done without armor and between exclusively noble parties. As this new type of fencing took hold, the weapons themselves evolved with it.

The name "rapier" most likely comes from the Spanish term *espada ropera* or "dress sword", first encountered in 1468.[14] It refers to a weapon that is worn in civilian contexts as opposed to those worn as part of military dress. As noted before, it is rather hard to pin down an exact specification for what is referred to as a rapier in history. The rapier we're dealing with in this book is the rapier influenced by Agrippa's new type of fencing at the peak of duelling in the late 1500s and early 1600s.[15]

Ridolfo Capoferro, in his 1610 fencing manual,[16] recommends that a rapier be so long as to have its point rest on the ground, while the pommel rests in the wielder's armpit when standing erect, giving us a sword that was as much as 12 to 20 inches longer than its predecessors. Swords of similar lengths appear in other Italian manuals of the era, including those of Nicoletto Giganti[17] (1606), Salvator Fabris[18] (1606), and Francesco Alfieri[19] (1640).

The length of the rapier allows the point itself to be used as a primary mode of defence, simply through threat. These longer rapiers also featured much more complex hilts than earlier swords with rings and bars surrounding the hand of the wielder. The "swept" and "cup" hilts gave the wielder greater protection in thrusting actions, especially those conducted simultaneously as both defence and attack. This mode of combined offence and defence became the norm in Italian fencing texts of the late 1500s, and throughout the 1600s, and replaced an earlier preference for two-time actions, where a defence would first be made and then followed by an offence.[20]

Though not all rapiers were exceedingly long, a weapon with a more complex hilt and thrusting-oriented profile became the norm amongst fencing masters throughout Europe.[21] In a challenge with a single opponent, there was no need to have your weapon immediately free after an attack. The weapons and armour of your opponent were also more consistent, meaning the rapier could give up the versatility required of battlefield weapons and become highly specialized.

The rapier, as it emerged in this period, was one of Europe's most deadly weapons in a one-on-one encounter. It was a weapon that developed out of revolutions in military thought and scholastic advancement, and captured the hearts and minds of a noble class obsessed with honor and valor.

Combined offence and defence. From the manual of Ridolfo Capoferro, 1610.

Wounding with the Rapier

The rapier wounds in two primary fashions: the thrust, and the cut.

Most of the techniques for the rapier are optimized for aligning your body behind a thrust, and for defending you against the thrusts of your opponent.

It only takes approximately 4 lbs (1.8 kilos) of pressure to push a sharp sword through human skin,[22] and it takes not much more to go through most clothing, except thick hides and real armor. When you deliver a thrust only a small amount of speed and intention is required to create the necessary force, and the impact is essentially imperceptible to the wielder.[23]

A thrust. Note that the back foot, lead knee, and point align. The back leg and sword hand also align.

The rapier syllabus contains many cutting techniques as well and the heavier and broader the sword you are using the more potent the cut. Cuts with the rapier are delivered by first withdrawing the sword, to prepare it, and then striking directly with the edge or by sending the end of the blade through a circle. The path of the cut meets and passes through its target, striking with a section of blade approximately 6 inches from the point. At this place the weapon has enough substance to cleave or slice and is accelerating fast enough to impart significant damage.

The preparation of a cut. Note the cut's eventual path.

In all fencing and practice we strike with care and precision. Even though the swords are blunted it is easy to accidentally hurt a friend through careless or overly fast movement. Focus your practice on alignment, intention, and timing. Bring speed into the equation only once you have established a solid foundation in your skills.

A Unified Approach

The system of rapier fencing that has developed at Academie Duello has come from years of study, practical experimentation, and competition. Its origins rest in the Italian systems of rapier taught and set down in manuals by historical masters, including Camillo Agrippa (1553), Salvator Fabris (1606), Nicoletto Giganti (1606), Ridolfo Capoferro (1610), and Francesco Alfieri (1640).

Academie Duello's system is not a re-creation of any one particular style, but instead follows the principles and strategies laid out by these masters and others who taught rapier in Italy at the height of its use and development. There are many more commonalities between these authors than there are differences, and it has proven to me to be a far more complete experience to present a unified approach to Italian fencing rather than trying to isolate one master's particular expression.

As modern practitioners we start with a very different base of knowledge and approach to learning than our historical forbearers. This makes historical texts not as easily accessible or comprehensible as we would like, especially for the first-time practitioner. My goal is to transmit the principles of Italian fencing to a modern reader in as efficient and effective a manner as possible based on who we are as modern people. And like the fencing masters of history, my goal is to give you an understanding of swordplay itself, not a scholastic understanding of a particular historical system.

Every technique that you learn in this book is based not only within the Italian tradition but is also described from a fundamental understanding. I do not teach any technique based on its placement in a historical text, instead I teach it based on its mechanical efficacy, its tactical context, and its strategic effectiveness. Essentially if I can't pull it off in combat, and teach others to consistently do the same, it's not ready to be part of my system. In this way I believe I can teach you to be an owner of the techniques you practice and give you a better chance of truly learning the art that lives underneath them.

It is important that you understand that the pedagogical approach, including some of the terms used here, as well as the use of some historical terms, are my own. Language is a powerful tool and I have used it to the best of my ability to transmit this art; that has meant adding terms and, more specifically, applying new theoretical and pedagogical ideas where I felt they added clarity. To help readers understand these differences, and apply what they learn here to their reading of historical sources, I have included a glossary of terms at the end that gives a comparison to historical usage. I have also provided endnotes regarding new terms and ideas, where appropriate, throughout the text. It's important to note that, especially when working with historical texts, the usage of terms varies broadly between authors.

Structures of the Art

If we were to imagine the art of swordplay as a metaphorical building it's structure would look something like this:

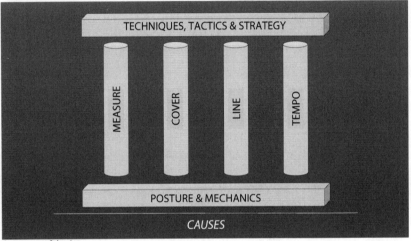

Structures of the Art.

Causes

Causes are the ground upon which an art is built; it's context, the reasons for it to exist as it does. There are potentially dozens of types of causes but a few include:

- **Combative Goals.** Is this an art designed to kill, win tournaments, subdue opponents, avoid conflict, all of the above?
- **Cultural Environment.** Are there laws or rules that the art needs to follow? Are there social pressures that define what is acceptable, attractive, or valuable?
- **Physical Environment.** Where does the art need to be applied? Is it used for self-defence on city streets, in multi-person melees, in one-on-one duels, or in multiple types of environments, or just in one?
- **Tools.** What is the nature of the weapons? Are they sharp and hewing or blunt and bludgeoning? Are they designed for scoring points or taking lives? If you're using a blunted edge weapon, is that the end of the road or is it standing in as a training tool for its sharp counterpart?

It's useful when looking at any art to understand where it comes from and where it's trying to take its practitioners. We call our foundational causes the *three tenets* (more on them momentarily).

Posture and Mechanics

How you hold and move your body is the foundation of the art. How you connect yourself with the ground, align your body and the weapon, and move to create power and structural strength. It is only upon a solid physical base that you can enact the combative principals of the art (the four pillars) and put into practice technique.

As in any martial art, a big part of being successful requires strength, range of motion, and conditioning. If you can't hold and move your body effectively it's difficult to implement combative strategies and accomplish combative objectives. Don't let that intimidate you. Anything athletic and unfamiliar is difficult and awkward at the beginning. Posture and mechanics is not only the place you start but a place you will return to refine as you improve.

Measure, Cover, Line, and Tempo

The four pillars of fencing are the principals upon which all of the techniques, tactics, and strategies of the art are based and must rely:

Measure - The judgment of distance between you and your opponent.
Cover - The management of safety from your opponent's weapons.
Line - The identification and creation of openings for attack.
Tempo - The understanding of timing, rhythm, and speed, and their relationship to distance.

Everything you try to do in fencing can be assessed through these pillars: What range do I need to be at to do this (measure)? How does it make me safe (cover)? How does it allow me to strike or setup a strike (line)? When is the right time to do it (tempo)?

Techniques, Tactics and Strategy

Upon good mechanics, and through adherence to the principles of the four pillars, we place the techniques, tactics, and strategy of the art.

This ground up structure is the approach that this book takes. We start with an orientation to the underlying causes and history of this art (chapter 1). Then we explore the foundational mechanics for the rapier and the techniques surrounding the pillar of measure in the chapters on Posture (chapter 2), Attack & Measure (chapter 3), and Movement (chapter 4). In the chapters on Gaining the Sword (chapter 5), Approaching Different Guards (chapter 6), Recovering Control (chapter 7), and Defence (chapter 8), you will learn the techniques of cover and line. The pillar of tempo is explored in-depth in chapter 9 where the previous techniques are pulled together and placed into the right moments of combat. Finally we'll dive into Strategy (chapter 10) and how to take skills From Drill to Combat (chapter 11).

The Three Tenets

At the founding of Academie Duello we asked ourselves whether our goal in the practice and teaching of these martial arts was re-creation or revival.

Re-creation is a historical and scholarly study whereby one attempts to translate, interpret, and practice the exact system set down by a historical master. In a re-creation environment great pains are taken to stay within the interpretation of a particular historical master and system and should our knowledge of that system change so must our art.

Revival also works with the teachings of historical masters but the focus is to use this knowledge to inform and develop a modern and evolving martial art that has historical roots. As a revival school, which was the choice we made, the goal is to stand on the shoulders of those who came before. To be as their students and to practice the art both as it was and as it could be.

The first challenge we faced was to create an environment that would help preserve and encourage the martial and historic aspects of the art we teach while allowing it room to grow. This led us to the establishment of three guiding principles: the Tenets. Through adherence to these tenets we believe that a group of passionate sword fighters locked in a room for 20 years of regular sparring and practice, with no outside influence, would develop techniques similar, if not exactly like, those of the masters in the Renaissance. The Tenets are:

Proper Arms

Always use the most accurate simulators of the weapons and armor for the martial art you are practicing.

The weapon is your first teacher. The techniques of the rapier are those that are optimal for the weight and balance of this particular weapon. Do not be surprised to find that the techniques of the modern Olympic epee are not best for the rapier, or that the techniques practiced with the bamboo shinai in Kendo are quite different from those practiced with the sharpened steel katana from which they were derived.

Proper Respect

Respect the deadliness of the weapons and the deadliness of an opponent using proper technique.

Though we practice and compete with blunted blades and do body to body work with control and care, it is important to always maintain awareness that the real weapon is sharp and contact with your opponent, or their weapon, potentially deadly. When you begin to see your weapon as a point scoring stick you will stop practicing a martial art and start playing a game.

Proper Context

Create combative environments and conditions that are as close to the traditional environment as possible.

The rapier was born out of the duel and that is the environment we apply it to in our practice. This is a space where a single decisive wound could end the engagement and one's life is truly on the line. There is no armor, the terrain is generally open (though the surfaces may vary), and you are generally facing a single opponent who is similarly, though not necessarily uniformly, armed.

Using this Book

This book will help you build a general competency with the fundamentals of the Italian Rapier. It's difficult to do this alone, so I recommend reading it along with a friend or group of practice partners. It can be useful to read it first from cover to cover to familiarize yourself with my overall approach to this art. Then, to truly absorb the material, it will be important to spend time on each section and the exercises therein.

Within each chapter the content is divided into theory, lessons, and exercises, as well as tactical and strategic applications. I hope that, through this multi-tiered approach, you can build an understanding, apply it with a partner, exercise and drill the practice until it is in your motor-programming, and then use tactical and strategic exercises to put what you learn in context, as soon as possible.

To truly understand the rapier you will need to realize these skills in a combative environment. I recommend that you move toward tactical exercises and slow free-sparring (safe combat with protective gear) as soon as you have the basics under your belt. If you are interested to learn more about combative rules and conventions, skip to the last chapter.

This book is a primer on the fundamentals of this system. There is much more depth and many more techniques that I will explore in two forthcoming volumes. Look to those for advanced techniques, use of secondary weapons, and strategic approaches to diverse contexts and opponents.

Lastly, books are a great way to learn theory, but a dynamic art such as this benefits from an approach that includes text, video and, if possible, hands-on instruction. My *Introduction to Italian Rapier* DVD and the Duello.TV video website offer full-motion descriptions of every exercise contained here (and many more) and are an ideal companion resource for further comprehension. My school, Academie Duello, in Vancouver, Canada, also offers workshops and intensive programs designed for visitors. We also send instructors abroad to help enthusiasts build their practice through expert instruction.

Notes on Layout

We have endeavored to make the lessons and exercises in the book as intuitive and easy to follow as possible. That being said, here are a few bits of guidance to help you understand them better:

Throughout the text we include in-line images, like the following.

A view of the swords from your perspective.   *Your partner's view of the swords.*

You'll note that these images contain a few guiding marks:

Circled numbers (①②) that match the written steps in the exercise.

A 👁 indicates that this image is seen from the perspective of the main operator in the exercise (referred to in the text as "you").

A ↱ indicates that this image is seen from the perspective of the partner in the exercise (referred to in the text as "partner" or "opponent").

When you see 🎞 beside an exercise you'll know to look to the bottom of the page to find a **Timeline Sequence** summary of that exercise, shown in profile. Exact steps are not specified but these sequences generally show the entire exercise from the beginning to end with short captions. They're a good way to either preview or review a given technique.

First in sequence ▸▸   Next in sequence ▸▸   Last in sequence.

Many images and diagrams also contain arrows to indicate movement, highlight body alignment, or draw attention to specific elements. I hope that these are self-explanatory.

| Mastering the Rapier

The journey of the rapier is long and rewarding and will provide even the most gifted with new epiphanies for years.

The fundamental techniques are relatively few and are represented in a few simple postures and exercises. You can acquire these fundamentals quickly, at least superficially; however, developing a full understanding of the art, and the ability to apply it in diverse situations, will take you years of study.

To access all that this weapon has to offer you, and to maximize the effectiveness of your study, I recommend that you follow these guidelines:

Acquire accurate simulators

The weapon is your first teacher. Make sure that you have a practice rapier that is suited to your stature and accurately represents the real, and deadly, weapon.

Establish a Training Regimen

Take part in a weekly study group or class and make time on your own to practice regularly. Class time is where you learn new skills, mark their progress, and identify flaws that need to be worked on. Training on your own is where you build muscle memory, and develop strong fundamental movement through repetition and continuity. For serious study, practice for at least two hours three times per week. On all other days, commit to practice for at least five minutes. Short sessions are very easy to keep up with, no matter how hectic your life. If you've forgotten during the day, five minutes before bed is easy enough to squeeze in. It also ensures that you get the weapon into your hand each day and often breaks the inertia between you and a more intense study session.

Practice with decent people who inspire and challenge you

Good practice partners make all the difference. Good partners—the ones you should seek out—drill and fence to learn, to test themselves, and for the joy inherent in those things. These people can challenge and inspire you. Bad partners drill and spar to win, to build their egos, and to prove something. Bad sparring partners can provide some small benefit when you are highly skilled, as some of them can provide a competitive challenge; however a complete lack of perspective beyond winning can suck the joy out of sparring, and learning, and lead to potentially dangerous situations.

Spar with intent and structure

Don't rush into sparring and don't get over-focused on winning. It is easy to develop poor habits and build techniques that only work against inexperienced sword fighters. I recommend sparring in a controlled environment with the objective of learning. Focus on applying given techniques, be observant of your form, and attempt to fence beautifully. Competition is fun and I encourage it; however, at the beginning you'll find it more useful to use competitive games, and other types of structured encounters, to allow you to build true proficiency with the fundamentals.

Teach

Having to take something you are doing intuitively and present it in a form that others can acquire will challenge and deepen your understanding. Most of my intermediate students have made their biggest strides toward deeper comprehension when they have begun teaching. However, as Achille Marozzo in his 1536 *Opera Nova* warned, do not over-represent your skills to yourself or your students and risk becoming an "Imperfect Master". Wait until you have a firm grounding in the art before becoming a teacher.

Work with sharp swords

Obviously not on your fellow training partners—instead work with "live" blades in exercises against test cutting objects, or even well-dressed pieces of meat such as pork or beef-sides. This will help you better understand what the rapier does well, and what it does poorly, as well as how to properly execute a technique to deadly effect.

Seek out an instructor of competence and worth

Though books like this are now readily available, as well as many historical treatises, truly excelling at an art is best done under the guidance of an instructor who can assess and analyze your progress, point you in new directions, and facilitate your learning.

Note on Left-Handed Fencing

For many reasons, it is most advisable to learn all sorts of weapon-play with either hand, and to develop the ability to strike and parry with the right or the left hand. - Antonio Manciolino, *Opera Nova*, 1531.

Every fencer should practice with both their dominant hand and their non-dominant hand. In fact the easiest time to develop your fencing ambidexterity is at the beginning, when both sides of your body are equally unconditioned. If you do not equally practice on both sides you will develop your body and mind unevenly.

Functionally and tactically it can be advantageous to develop martial arts from both sides. Some studies have shown that symmetrically-developed martial artists employ greater diversity in their combative approaches and are more successful, in some competitive environments, because of this.[24]

Uneven body development can also lead to health problems, as the one-sided development in the muscles of your shoulder and hips can bring your bones out of alignment, pinch nerves, and cause other issues.[25] Uneven mental development simply makes for a less competent sword fighter, especially when you get to the point where you're using two weapons simultaneously. If you let one side gain significant endurance over the other you will find that playing catch-up takes a lot of discipline; You will always want to favor the hand that is easier and feels fresher. Balance the time you spend between both hands at the beginning and you'll be happier, and more competent, in the long run.

If you or a training partner are left-handed, then train symmetrically at first. Meaning, if you are using your left hand have your partner do the same and then have both of you spend time on the right. Once you have gained proficiency with swordplay in a symmetrical environment you can start exploring how you can adapt to asymmetrical situations, where one fencer is left-handed and the other right.

For clarity, in this book I present all of the exercises and images showing right-handed fencers. I endeavour to use the term "sword-side" to refer to the dominant side and "off-hand side", or "off-side," to refer to the side where you are not holding a sword, as much as possible, to make things easier for left-handed fencers as much as right. There are, however, times when simply right and left are best. Pay close attention to the pictures and descriptions when translating a given technique from the right to the left hand.

Equipment

To practice the art correctly, you will need equipment that properly simulates the historical tools of the art. Fortunately, equipment is much more readily accessible now than it was 10 or 15 years ago. Many choices exist on the market for both armor and weapons. The gamut ranges from inexpensive and serviceable to high-quality and premium-priced.

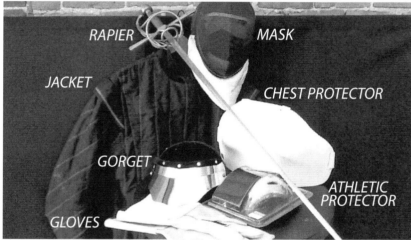

RAPIER MASK

JACKET CHEST PROTECTOR

GORGET

GLOVES ATHLETIC PROTECTOR

Clockwise: A rapier, mask, chest protector, athletic protector, gloves, gorget, and jacket.

Protective Equipment

Pairs drilling is best done with, at least, the following protective equipment:

- A "three-weapons" fencing mask
- A gorget/throat-protector, made of steel or rigid leather.
- Comfortable footwear and workout clothing. A good running shoe with a flexible bottom is important. Wrestling shoes, indoor running shoes, fencing shoes (available online), and even Kendo shoes, offer the protection of footwear with the flexibility of a bare foot. If you have a good and safe training floor, doing your drills barefoot is an excellent way to strengthen your feet.

For sparring, I recommend the following additional equipment:

- A padded combat jacket made for rapier fencing.
- Gloves. At Duello we use motorcycle gloves as they provide good durability, comfort, and a cuff that offers protection to the wrist.

The Rapier

Historical rapiers varied in dimension both throughout their evolution from the early 1500s to the 1700s and within any given period, based on the usage and physical size of their wielders. As mentioned before, different masters advocated differing weights, lengths, and balances. The swords shown in Agrippa's 1553 manual are shorter in blade than those of later authors, at about one and a half arm lengths (when compared to his models). In perhaps the peak of the Italian rapier era (the early 1600s), Capo Ferro, Giganti, and Fabris show blades of at least two arm lengths.

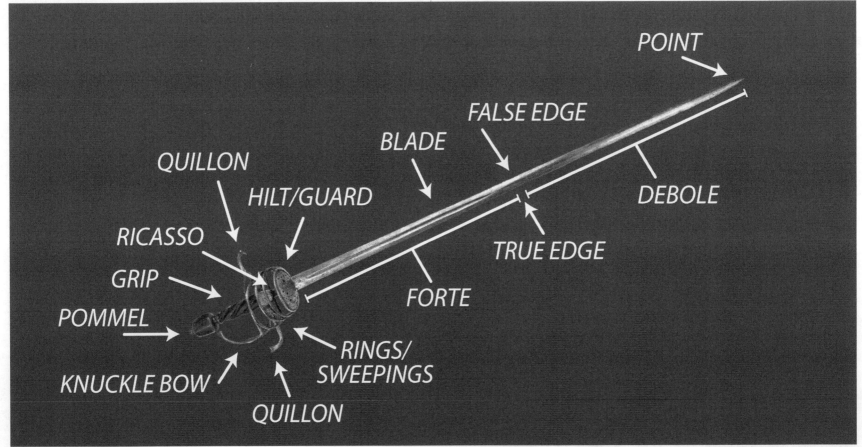

The parts of a 17th century rapier.

However, some contemporaries to these authors, such as Vincentio Saviolo (his manual published in 1595), show images with rapiers that are broader bladed and potentially even longer. In museum collections relating to rapiers of the early 1600s you can find examples that range in overall length between 40" to 70". We also know that blade length restrictions were brought into many European cities, most notably London in 1566 when a young Queen Elizabeth restricted the blade length of rapiers to approximately 40" (one yard and half-a-quarter).[26] This was perhaps a statement of support for the shorter and more English broadsword, and backsword, and against duelling, which was a more continental fashion often done with rapiers.

In my experience, rapiers have a surprisingly broad range of weights from as light as two pounds to as heavy as five and half. The weight can be from the blade itself or based on the weight and complexity of the hilt and pommel. In a study by Florian Fortner and Julian Schrattenecker that compared 7 historical rapiers to modern reproduction swords, their studied examples had a range in weight between 1130 g (2.5 lbs) and 1630 g (3.5 lbs) and thickness at the ricasso ranged between 8.3mm and 10.3mm and width between 14.7 mm and 24.4 mm.[27] Often what makes a blade feel heavy or light is where on its length you find its center of balance (the point where you can balance the rapier and it will hold an equilibrium between its hilt and point). Rapiers in the study had balance points from 3.7" to 6.1" from the hilt.

Careful examination of sword hilts in rapier manuals varies from simple cross bars and rings around the fingers to much more complex hilts that include sweeps and plates on both sides of the blade.

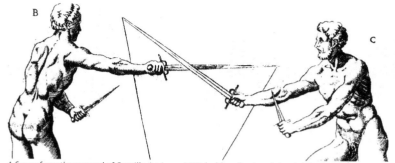

A figure from the manual of Camillo Agrippa, 1553, holds a short and simple hilted rapier.

The rapiers in the manual of Salvator Fabris, 1606, are long and feature complex hilts.

Ridolfo Capo Ferro in his 1610 manual advocated that a rapier's length be from armpit to floor when standing erect.

The Right Rapier for You

An important thing emphasized both by historical masters and this author is that your rapier should suit your build and your capabilities.

Length certainly has the advantage of being able to reach farther but it can also be much more challenging to maneuver and presents a much longer lever to your opponent. Though I work with rapiers as long as those advocated by Capo Ferro, I think having a rapier whose quillons (crossbar) come up to your belly button, when the point is resting on the floor, provides a good and manageable length for most practitioners (typically a blade between 36" and 45").

The rapier system I present is best suited for more slender, thrusting oriented, weapons that are between 2 and 4 lbs in overall weight with complex hilts (sweepings or rings). I recommend that you have a balance point along the blade of between 2 and 5 inches from the hilt. If the balance point is too far back into the handle your sword will be easily pushed around by your opponent.

Ensure that the blade is flexible enough not to hurt too much when you strike but firm enough not to wobble when you move it through the air or interact with another weapon.

A good test for a rapier's flexibility is to hold the sword by the grip and place the sword against a home scale. Apply about two pounds of pressure. The blade should bend off the centerline between one and two inches. Preferably this bend will occur in the third of the blade closest to the point, which is the focal point for striking with the weapon.

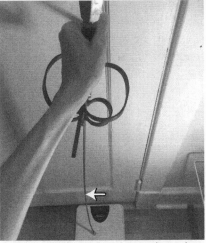

You can also get a feel for the blade by maneuvering it through the air or attempting to cause the blade to wobble. If the blade oscillates excessively or, when held straight with the flat towards the ground, bends more than a small degree under the weight of its own point, it is probably too flexible for effective use.

Two inches of deflection from the centerline under two pounds of pressure on a bathroom scale.

At Academie Duello we use rebated rapier blades made by several different makers, notably: CAS Iberia/Hanwei, Darkwood Armory, Del Tin Armi Antiche, and Marco Danelli. On the end of the rapier we affix an archery blunt, which is a rubber stopper, you can typically find at archery supply stores or order online.

Equipment, and its makers, change all the time. I recommend you take a look at my website for an updated list of my recommendations for swords and protective equipment as well as for discount starter kits for readers of this book:

http://www.academieduello.com/equipment

Chapter Two

Those who like the guards, and counterguards, and constraining, here, there, above, and below, feints, and counterfeints, slope paces, voids of the legs, and crossings, must necessarily form and move their bodies in many strange ways; which, as things done by chance and that were founded without reasons that are sound and true, we will leave to their authors.

—Ridolfo Capoferro, *Gran Simulacro dell'Arte e dell'uso di Schermire,* 1610

POSTURE

Posture, and our physical structure, is the base upon which all good martial art sits. To be effective your weapon needs to feel like an extension of your body and your body an extension of the ground. In this section you will learn how to hold the sword, properly place your body for attack and defence, and move effectively between the core postures.

Natural, Comfortable, and Optimal

When approaching rapier fencing, and many other martial arts, I have often heard practitioners advise a new student to do whatever feels "natural" to them. This idea then typically leads to a new student developing a poor foundation for their long-term success.

We often confuse the idea of what feels "comfortable" with what truly is natural. Comfort is the feeling we get from the long-term repetition of a particular activity or posture. In time we can become comfortable with nearly anything, whether it is good for our body's health or not and whether it is in-line with our goals or counter to them. Think of the hunched posture many of us develop from sitting at a desk for many hours at a time; it may feel comfortable but it's certainly not natural.

For something to be "natural" it must be in alignment with nature, in this case, that means the structure and composition of the human body. A natural movement, or position, would be well supported by our skeletal structure, in-line with the movement of our joints, work well with our muscles to create grace and stability, and help our circulatory system do its job.

Every position that you will learn in this book is natural in these ways and is also optimal for the goals that you want to achieve when you have a rapier in your hand.

An optimal rapier posture will:

• Guard your safety by presenting a deadly threat to your opponent.

• Restrict the targets that your opponent can strike.

• Place your sword in its most tactically advantageous place.

• Align your body for strength, stability, and speed.

Developing a highly optimized posture will help you to achieve the highest level of rapier fencing and will expand your body's natural capabilities. Comfort will come in time through thoughtful and regular practice.

Holding the Sword

A firm and sensitive connection with your sword will allow you to:
- Apply the force of your whole body through the weapon.
- Resist the force of your opponent's sword.
- Maneuver with precision and ease.
- Maximize the endurance of your wrist and arm.
- Make optimal body and sword positions with comfort and ease.

If you have a weak or improper connection with the sword you will find that your wrist or hand gets tired quickly (even after you've been practicing with the rapier for several months), and that certain positions of the sword, and arm, are challenging, or even painful, to form. You will also find that your opponent can easily push your blade around and thus strike through your defence.

Pay careful attention to how you hold your sword and revisit the ideas presented in this section frequently as you progress. To hold your sword:

① Hold your rapier in your off-hand by its forte. Place it comfortably in front of you, so you can easily access its handle with your sword-hand, with the knuckle-bow toward the ground.

② Place your sword-hand palm-down over the sword's handle with your index finger reaching past the quillon and your remaining fingers over the handle. The handle of the rapier should run diagonally across your palm with the pommel at the heel of your hand and the ricasso at the second knuckle of your index finger.

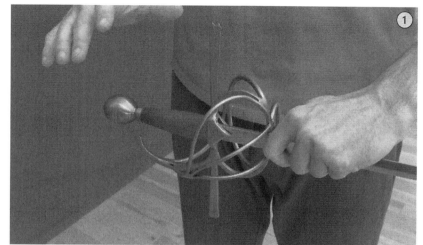

Hold the rapier by its forte.

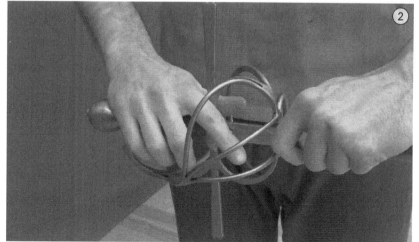

Grasp the handle with your index finger past the quillon.

③ Hook your index finger, at the farthest knuckle, around the ricasso. Have the rest of your fingers comfortably grasp the handle. Place your thumb on the opposite side of the ricasso, on the same side of the quillons as your finger tips. Point your thumb toward the tip of the rapier.

④ Place the handle under your palm.

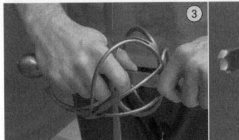

Comfortably grasp the handle and ricasso.

The sword's orientation across the palm, as shown from below.

A correct grip:

- Requires only the index finger and the pommel against the heel of your hand to keep it's point up.
- Aligns the bones of your arm with your true edge, allowing you to apply a strong downward force using your entire body.
- Can resist a downward force from your opponent's rapier.

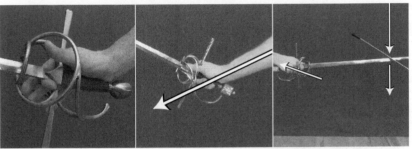

The sword's handle rests against the hand. The point is held up through leverage.

The handle and pommel are underneath the forearm.

Pressure against the back of the blade is taken into the hand.

Tips

- Always stay as relaxed as possible in your grip.
- Only use as much strength as is necessary to conduct a given action.
- Movement of your rapier's blade and point should be conducted through the manipulation of the fingers, and wrist, with the thumb directing the point.
- Use as little upper arm motion as possible.

Positioning the Lower Body

Imagine a straight line, that runs on the ground, between you and your opponent. This is the "line of direction".

① With your feet form an L shape on the *line of direction*. Place your *sword-side* foot in front. Point it at your opponent. Place your *off-side* foot behind it with your heel on the line.

② Rest your shoulders so they are in-line with your hips and turn your head to look along the *line of direction*. You will be presenting your *sword-side* shoulder to your opponent.

Form an "L" on the line of direction.

Shoulders align to the line of direction.

③ Advance your *sword-side* foot two foot-lengths, along the *line of direction*.

④ Bend your back leg, sliding your hips back, until your rear knee extends over your toes (but not past them). Take about 80% of your weight onto this leg.

⑤ Soften your front knee so it is not locked. Keep your weight over the balls of your feet with your heels resting lightly.

Step two foot lengths along the line of direction.

Take 80% of your weight over your back foot. Soft front knee.

The Defensive Posture

There are two formations of the sword and upper body. The *defensive posture* and *offensive posture*.[28] For clarity, I will describe these for a fencer holding their sword in their right hand.

To form the *defensive posture*:

① Position your feet as described before.

② Lean back slightly so that your head is drawn back over your left shoulder and your left breast is above your left buttock. Keep your left buttock over your left heel.

③ Place the forearm of your right arm, parallel with the floor, at the height of your waist. Leave one hand-span of distance between your elbow and your side.

④ Orient your *true edge* toward the ground and direct your sword's point toward the face of your opponent.

⑤ Place your left hand (your *off-hand*) beside your left cheek with your palm toward your face.

In the *defensive posture* your sword protects your flank with its *hilt*. Your head and legs are protected by being withdrawn, thus farther away, from the opponent's point.

The defensive posture: Head, chest, and leg are withdrawn.

The Offensive Posture

The *offensive posture* is both a waiting position, that presents a higher degree of threat, and a transition position, used when moving from the *defensive posture* into an attack.

To form the *offensive posture*:

① Form the *defensive posture*.

② Extend your sword toward your opponent. Straighten your arm until your hand is at the height of your shoulder.

③ Reach forward with your right shoulder so that your right breast is over the middle of your right thigh. Keep your body profiled and your hips back. You should maintain the 80/20 weight distribution between your rear foot and front foot.

In this position your head and chest are protected by the hilt of your sword while your lower body is protected through being withdrawn.

The bent back leg, in both postures, helps you keep targets away from your opponent and stores energy for an explosive attack.

The offensive posture: Weapon, arm, and shoulders are extended. Hips and leg are withdrawn

Off-hand Position

The *off-hand* (the one that is not holding your sword) can be used to defend yourself by pushing an opponent's sword out of the way, especially when your sword has failed to do so. There are two useful ready positions for your hand in the *defensive* or *offensive posture*.[29]

By the Face (Open Position)

Place the hand beside your *off-side* cheekbone, with the fingers extended by your eyes.

This facilitates an easy defence for the face by simply passing the palm across the face to the *sword-side*. It also sets up a defence for the upper torso by passing the forearm in front of the body.

The open position.

The off-hand parries by pushing across the face or body toward the sword-side.

By the Lead Arm (Closed Position)

Extend the *off-hand* to touch the sword arm, as far forward as comfortably possible without turning your shoulders.

The proximity of your *off-hand* to your sword-arm eliminates the ability of your opponent to strike your body between the sword and the *off-hand* (the reason it is called the "closed" position).

The closed position.

The off-hand parries by pushing across the body toward the off-hand side.

Tips Regarding Off-hand Position

- Keep your *off-hand* back or hidden behind your sword hilt. This will prevent it from being easily struck.
- Stay profiled, especially in the *closed position*. Reach forward with your *off-hand* as far as you can without squaring your shoulders and making your body a larger target.
- If you have a larger chest you may find it easier to place your arm over your chest rather than under or beside. To do this: reach straight up, then extend your arm forward and down, with a circular motion.

Placing the offhand over the chest to extend its reach.

Alignment Advice

- Keep your knees and toes oriented in the same direction.

Front toe and knee point in the same direction.   *Back toe and knee point in the same direction.*

- When you straighten your arm or leg keep the joint slightly bent ("soft"). Locking a joint can easily lead to hyper-extension.
- Keep your weight over the back leg as you move into the *offensive posture*.
- Keep your weight on the balls of your feet. This will help you stay balanced.
- Keep your front toe pointing at your opponent.

Keep your weight over the back leg.   *The front toe must point along the line of direction to the opponent.*

- Your rear toe should be oriented at 90-degrees to the front, or at a greater angle (for balance and knee alignment) up to 120 degrees.
- In the *defensive posture* keep your hips in-line with your chest and back heel. Do not let the *sword-side* hip push forward toward your opponent.

90-degree relationship between the front and back foot.   *120-degree relationship between the front and back foot.*   *Note the left hip is over the left foot.*

The Importance of Being Profiled

Look at the two fencers above. The fencer on the right is standing in a very square fashion, with the hips open and both shoulders forward. The fencer on the left is standing with their feet in an L shape, with their shoulders and hips over the *line of direction*. Which fencer is presenting the smaller target?

Hopefully, the answer to this is clear: the one on the left.

A large part of your defence relies on keeping your body behind your sword. By being well profiled you reduce the amount of movement required to keep your body safe.

Another common error made when forming the *offensive posture* is leaning the body to the left and off the *line of direction*. Instead, extend along the line to keep the body profiled.

Incorrect! The fencer is leaning off the line of direction.   *Correct! The fencer is extending forward along the line of direction.*

To stay as profiled as possible, be sure to keep your shoulders, hips, and feet over the *line of direction*.

This orientation of the body will feel difficult at first and certainly may feel uncomfortable. Time invested now will help you develop an excellent postural foundation for later sword-work. Be sure to use the exercises that follow to develop the strength and ability to make the optimal, profiled, posture.

Target Management

The *hilt* of your sword is its most defensive component. What is placed behind the *hilt* is generally protected by its *rings* and the *forte* of your blade. Though it may seem small, by pushing it toward the threat, it creates a much larger protective area I call the "cone of protection". This is similar to how a small object can make a large shadow by being close to the light source.

Those things that are not behind the *hilt* need to be protected through distance. The *defensive* and *offensive postures* are designed to use these two principles to restrict your opponent's ability to easily attack you.

In the *defensive posture* your flank is protected by your *hilt*. Your head and upper body are withdrawn to protect them through distance.

In the *offensive posture* the hilt and the threat of your point protect your upper body. Your lower body is withdrawn to protect it through distance.

The offensive posture (left) and defensive posture (right).

In the attack you push forward in the offensive posture. The hilt's placement extends the cone of protection and protects the head and upper body.

Note how Right's hilt pushes Left's sword away from their body.

Exercise: Postural Isolation ▦

The following exercise will help you develop body awareness and the ability to coordinate each part of your body while maintaining proper alignment of your shoulders and hips.

Throughout the exercise move only the body parts you are directed to move. Though later you will blend movements into a whole, at this point, you want to practice distinct, crisp, and isolated movement.

This exercise does not require a sword.

① Begin in the *offensive posture*, with your right side leading. Extend your left arm behind you, over the *line of direction*, and in-line with your right arm. Keep both arms parallel with the ground.

② Shift your hips forward, so your weight is over your right leg. Maintain the alignment of your arms throughout this shift.

③ Shift your shoulders back, so your left shoulder is in-line with your left foot. Maintain the position of your arms.

④ Shift your hips back so your weight is completely over the left leg. Maintain your upper body and arm alignment.

⑤ Shift your shoulders forward, reaching with your right hand out in front of your right side. Maintain your hips and weight over the left foot.

⑥ Repeat steps 2 to 5.

It is ideal, in this exercise, to have a partner observe you. You can also use a video camera to observe yourself. Look for the following signs that you are performing optimally:

- **Crisp** and distinct movement. For example, your hips will stay precisely in place while you reach forward with your shoulders.
- **Complete** each movement before the next movement begins. The goal is to not blend movements unintentionally.
- **Shoulders** over hips. **Hips** over feet. Watch for leaning and tilting of the body.
- **Arms** and shoulders parallel with the ground. Not higher or lower than the other.
- **Hips** stay the same distance from the ground as you propel them forward and backward. They do not rise or fall.
- **Knees** stay in alignment with toes. As you shift your weight forward the knee should stay over the foot and not drift to the inside.

▦ Reach shoulders forward ▸▸   Slide hips forward ▸▸   Reach shoulders back ▸▸   Slide hips back ▸▸   Repeat.

Chapter Three

Suppose two fencers meet – one very proficient in the thrust, the other in the cut. Rest assured that the first fencer would definitely come out the winner, even though the second fencer was a more physically powerful person.
—Salvator Fabris, *Lo Schermo*, 1606

ATTACK & MEASURE

Late 16th-century and early 17th-century rapiers are excellent thrusting weapons and can also create significant damage with a *cut*, if wielded properly and with sufficient momentum and force.

In a duelling context the *thrust* is by far the superior form of attack, because it strikes at the farthest distance with the lowest commitment. It also keeps the *hilt* and blade of the weapon in front of you as you attack, which will keep you safer.

The *cut*, though effective in many contexts, risks exposing your body as it passes its target. It is also harder to strike an effective wounding blow with a lighter-bladed weapon, such as the rapier.

In this section you'll learn how to attack with the *thrust* and explore the various ranges of attack, known as the five *measures*.

32 | Five Measures

"Measure" or *misura* (Italian) is the distance between your point and your opponent's body, and your opponent's point and your body. Being able to judge how far you are from your opponent is vital for choosing the correct technique to apply and understanding the level and type of threat that you are facing.

There are five *measures*, each defined by the length and type of motion required to strike the opponent's body with a *thrust*. They are:

① *Fuori Misura (Out of Measure)*. Beyond the distance from which you can strike or be struck in a single movement.

② *Misura Larghissima (Widest Measure)*. The distance of your longest range attack, the *passing lunge*, where your back foot must pass your front foot.

③ *Misura Larga (Wide Measure)*. The distance from which you can strike by moving only your front foot.

④ *Misura Stretta (Narrow Measure)*. The distance from where you can strike without moving your feet, simply by going into the *offensive posture* and shifting your weight.

⑤ *Misura Strettissima (Narrowest Measure)*. The distance where you can strike by moving sharply into the *offensive posture*.

To help build up the fundamental body mechanics of thrusting, we're going to start from *misura strettissima* and work our way out. You can then re-explore the *measures* by starting, as you would in combat, from *fuori misura* (out of measure) and working your way back in.

Note that the terms I use here, as well as those in various historical sources, differ from one another. Refer to the notes on historical usage and glossary in the appendix for more information.

A Note on Friendly Thrusting

The goal with a sharp rapier is to put the point at least two inches into the opponent to properly wound. In some historical sources you'll see images where the rapier goes as much as one to two feet through a target. So when assessing your measure in a true duelling situation you need to accommodate for the penetration required to do the damage you seek to do.

An image from the manual of Nicoletto Giganti that shows an approximately 1 foot penetration through the opponent's chest.

In a practice situation, however, you want to accommodate for the health and safety of your training partners. Though modern practice rapiers are flexible, being struck forcefully over and over again can really reduce your desire to train in a prolonged fashion. In general practice, aim to the surface of your partner's skin instead of aiming through their body. Seek to strike in a way that is firm but not hard or overly painful.

Fuori Misura.

Misura Larga.

Misura Stretta.

Misura Strettissima.

Misura Larghissima.

Striking from Misura Strettissima

At *misura strettissima* you can strike your opponent with no more than a straightening of your arm and extension from the *defensive posture* into the *offensive posture*.

The Strettissima Thrust

① Start in the *defensive posture*, directing your point at the target.

② Extend your sword arm.

③ Sharply push your shoulders forward, bending at your flank, striking your opponent as you extend into the *offensive posture*.

Be sure not to shift your weight forward from your back leg. This is a very short range attack.

Defensive posture.

Extend arm

Push shoulders forward.

Striking from Misura Stretta

At *misura stretta* you can strike your opponent by changing into the *offensive posture* and shifting your weight forward. This action is known as a *firm-footed lunge*.

The Firm-Footed Lunge

① Start in the *defensive posture,* directing your point at the target.

② Extend your sword and upper body into the *offensive posture.*

③ Sharply straighten your back leg. Shift your weight over your front foot and strike with the extended sword. Keep your hips level with the ground throughout the movement, as if they were on a track. The knee of your lead leg extends over your front toe and no further.

Defensive posture.

Offensive posture.

Shift hips forward.

To recover:

① Return your knee to its original position to draw the hips back. Leave your upper body in the *offensive posture*. Keep your head hidden behind the *hilt* of your sword.

② Return the upper body to the *defensive posture* by withdrawing the shoulders and then the arm.

The order of operations in this action is vital. By extending your sword first you immediately present a threat to your opponent. This forces them to deal with the threat before they can deal with you. Pushing the upper body forward into the *offensive posture* then creates alignment for a powerful attack and optimal protection (by placing your *hilt* in front of your head, and keeping your other vital targets away). Once you have created the *offensive posture*, and know that the way is safe, you then propel yourself forward with the back leg.

The withdrawing order is just as important; you want to make sure that your body stays aligned behind your sword and its most defensive parts, as long as possible, until you can use distance to protect you.

Withdraw hips first.

Withdraw shoulders and lower sword.

Striking from Misura Larga

Misura larga is the distance where you need to advance your front foot to strike your opponent in the body with a thrust. This type of attack is known as a *lunge*. It is one of the most common forms of attack with the rapier.

The Lunge

① Begin in the *defensive posture,* directing your point at the target.

② Extend your sword and upper body into the *offensive posture*. Be sure to keep the hips retired and your weight over your back leg.

③ Sharply straighten your back leg, pushing forcefully against the ground with your whole foot. Step one foot-length forward with the front foot and push your hips over your front leg. Extend the lead knee so it is over the lead toe and no further. Be sure to keep the back foot flat on the ground. Do not allow the heel to lift or the foot to slide.

④ Extend the *off-hand* behind you while making the step, and align the shoulders and back arm over the *line of direction*. This provides a counterbalance to the sword, maximizes reach, and reduces target area.

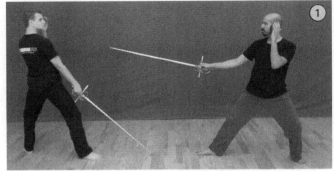

Defensive posture.

Offensive posture.

Lunge.

To recover:

① Bend the back knee to draw the hips back. Leave your upper body in the *offensive posture*. Keep your head hidden behind the *hilt* of your sword.

② Push off the ball of your front foot, and while your hips begin to shift, pull the foot and hips back to their original position. Recover the *off-hand* into guard position.

③ Return the upper body to the defensive posture by withdrawing the shoulders and then the arm.

Recover the hips and foot.

Recover shoulders then arm.

Mechanics and Tips

The *lunge* is designed to be a safe and fast method of attack. Proper order of the *lunge* is essential, as well as strong alignment of the body. The goal is to keep your vital parts hidden behind your sword and your muscles, and structure, aligned for the strongest and most powerful attack.

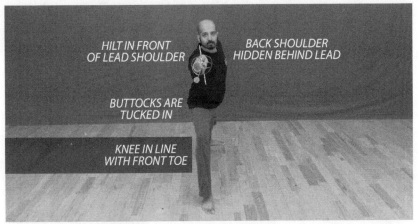

HILT IN FRONT
OF LEAD SHOULDER

BACK SHOULDER
HIDDEN BEHIND LEAD

BUTTOCKS ARE
TUCKED IN

KNEE IN LINE
WITH FRONT TOE

A proper lunge as seen from the front.

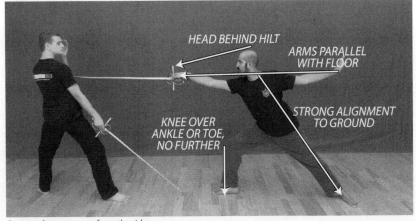

HEAD BEHIND HILT

ARMS PARALLEL
WITH FLOOR

STRONG ALIGNMENT
TO GROUND

KNEE OVER
ANKLE OR TOE,
NO FURTHER

A proper lunge as seen from the side.

Present the Threat First

Make sure not to lead an attack with your face. Send the sword out ahead of your body by using proper order in the *lunge*:

① Sword and arm

② Shoulders

③ Hips and feet.

Keep the head safe throughout the recovery by following the opposite order: hips and feet, then shoulders, then finally sword and arm.

Incorrect! Right did not present his sword first so he was struck before his attack could land.

Make a Short Crisp Step

Keep your step short and sudden (one foot-length is a good balance between quickness and reach). The longer the step the more risk to you. There is no way to retreat while your foot is in the air.

Keep the proper distance between your feet in your initial stance so that a shorter stepping *lunge* still reaches a long way.

Be sure not to drag your feet when lunging or recovering. This will slow down both actions and potentially trip you up on rough terrain. Push off the ball of the front foot when recovering to stop the heel from dragging.

Incorrect! Don't allow the heel to drag.   *Correct! Pick up the whole foot as you recover.*

Strike with Your Body, Not Your Arm

Maintain the extension of the arm all the way through the *lunge*. Your body is the driving force behind the *thrust*. Resist the urge to withdraw and then "pump" the arm while stepping. This might feel more forceful but greater force is not required to be effective. Withdrawing the arm delays your attack and reduces your safety.

Incorrect! Right withdrew his arm as he attacked exposing his head.   *Correct! Right has fully extended his arm and shoulders before lunging.*

Striking from Misura Larghissima: Sword Leading

Misura larghissima is the most extreme distance from which you can strike, using an attack called a *passing lunge*.

There are two ways to conduct the *passing lunge*:

1. Sword leading. The hips stay in their same orientation as you pass forward. This keeps your right shoulder forward and your sword closer to the opponent.

2. *Off-side* leading. The hips turn, bringing the *off-hand*, and shoulder, closer to the opponent.

Generally, when working with sword alone, it is best to favour the first type of passing lunge which leaves the sword more dominantly in position to defend you.

① Start in the *defensive posture*, directing your point at the target.

② Extend your sword and upper body into the *offensive posture*.

③ Shift your weight onto your lead foot.

Defensive posture.

Offensive posture.

Shift weight forward.

④ Step with the back foot past the lead and slightly to the left of the *line of direction* (not directly in front of the foot). Maintain the orientation of the feet and hips so (for a right handed fencer) your right foot continues to point forward while your left foot continues to point out to your left As you begin the step, extend the *off-hand* behind you and align the shoulders and back arm over the *line of direction*.

⑤ Land on the foot with the knee bent and your body supported over your new front leg. Your back leg (the right leg if your sword is in your right hand) should be extended, with the ball of the foot resting on the ground, with the heel lifted.

Begin the pass.

Conclude the passing lunge.

Note the foot orientation.

Striking from Misura Larghissima: Off-Side Leading

As you develop further in your skill you may find times when bringing forward your *off-hand* or a secondary item, such as a dagger or shield, can be advantageous for your defence.

① Start in the *defensive posture*, directing your point at the target.

② Extend your sword and upper body into the *offensive posture* while turning your *sword-hand* palm-down (this rotates your arm and shoulder into a more natural position for the next part of the movement). Reach forward with your *off-hand* placing it just below the elbow of your *sword-arm*. Let the reaching of your *off-hand* begin to turn your shoulders and hips.

③ Shift your weight onto your lead foot, push off your back foot, and step your back foot past the lead foot. Continue the turning of your shoulders and hips so that your *off-side* comes ahead of your *sword-side* as you step.

Defensive posture.

Bring offhand forward.

Shift weight forward.

④ Turn on the ball of the lead foot (your right, if your sword is in your right hand) so that it is 90 degrees to its original position. If your sword is in your right hand, your right foot will now point to your right. The passing foot (your left, if your sword is in your right hand), should land, in front, pointed toward the opponent along the *line of direction*.

⑤ Your attack ends with your new front knee over your toes, your weight carried over the front leg, and your body turned so that your chest faces toward your sword side. Your body should be profiled behind your sword with the *off-side* leading and your *off-hand* beneath your *sword-arm*. This adds the protection of your *off-hand* to that of your sword.

Note foot orientation.

Conclude the passing lunge.

Recovering from a Passing Lunge

There are two methods of recovery:

1. Continue the pass forward into a second, lead-leg, *lunge*.

Bring the right foot forward past the left.

Conclude with a lead-leg lunge, through the opponent.

2. Pass backward and recover in good order: hips and feet, shoulders, and then sword.

Pass the right leg back behind the left.

Return to the offensive posture before going to the defensive posture.

Reorient the hips, if they are turned, as you pass forward into the new *lunge* or recover back into the *defensive posture*.

Out of Measure

It is from this safe place that a duel should begin. Here you are beyond the reach of your opponent's ability to strike you, even with their most extreme attack. However, you are also beyond your own reasonable striking distance.

This *measure* is particularly important not to misjudge. Here you can safely analyze your opponent and make plans before you approach.

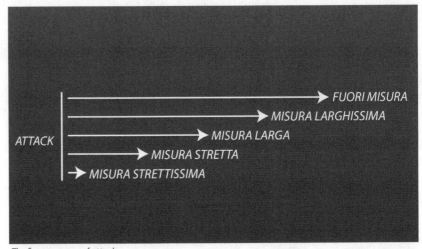

The five measures of attack.

Lunging Measure Drill

You can develop your sense of *measure* by attacking targets at varying *measures*. As a solo drill, place a series of objects in-line with one another at different distances. This could be a series of tennis balls suspended from the ceiling, or a series of targets on a tabletop placed at the various *measures*.

Practice striking the different targets using only the attack required for the appropriate *measure*. If you make a *lunge* but discover you could have struck with a *firm-footed lunge* (larga vs stretta), attempt the exercise again with a shorter attack. Each attack flows one into the other, so if you start with a *firm-footed lunge*, you can transform it mid-motion into a full *lunge*.

Practice the same exercise again, approaching or retreating from each target in order to always be at a given *measure*. For example, always working to be in the perfect lunging distance of *misura larga*.

A partner can help you in this exercise by presenting a hand as a target. After you appropriately strike a target, your partner can then move their hand to a closer or farther position. This will challenge you to rejudge your measure and select the appropriate *thrust*.

The most important thing in these exercises is to make sure that your movements are crisp and well balanced. It is far better to fall short of a target, but be poised in a well structured *lunge*, than to fall all over yourself overreaching for a target whose *measure* you misjudged.

Right strikes Left's hand at misura stretta.

Right strikes Left's hand at misura larghissima.

Resistance Lunging ▤

The thrusting techniques in this section rely on a strong alignment of the body behind the attack. This exercise will help you develop proper structural and muscular alignment in all types of *thrusts*. It requires a partner but not a sword.

In the exercise you are going to conduct a *lunge* while your partner provides resistance through a connection with your sword arm. In this way you will be able to feel the connection from your weapon hand all the way to your back foot and into the ground. Through resistance you can discover and correct weaknesses in your alignment.

① Stand across from your partner and take the *defensive posture*. Place your sword arm and hand into its proper position and form a fist with your *sword-hand*.

② Have your partner stand in front of you and cup your *sword-hand* in both of their hands. They should prepare themselves to provide you with resistance by getting into a low and stable posture. Be sure to have a flush alignment between the back of your hand and forearm. Your partner may need to support your hand and wrist to help you maintain this alignment.

Support the wrist.

③ With your partner providing medium resistance, extend your hand, pushing your partner back, so your hand aligns with your shoulders.

④ Push your shoulders and arm forward into the *offensive posture*. Your partner will continue to resist through this stage and each subsequent stage.

⑤ Conduct a *lunge* into your partner, driving them back through the connection of your arm, pushing off the ground behind you. Your partner will move back as you push them forward, maintaining a constant resistance.

Lunge into your partner, pushing with the back leg.

▤ Take the defensive posture ▸▸ | Extend the hand ▸▸ | Push the shoulders forward ▸▸ | Conduct a lunge, pushing your partner back.

⑥ Bracing against the constant force of your partner, begin to recover from your lunge. Recover the foot and hips first.

⑦ Recover the shoulders.

⑧ Recover the upper body and then the arm. Maintain a constant speed and strong resistance to your partner throughout the recovery.

Begin by practicing this exercise with a slow and constant push forward. Once you have gained comfort and explored some of the errors presented next, add an explosive element where you attempt to throw your partner backward as you propel yourself forward in the *lunge*.

Recover the upper body and then the arm.

Begin to recover back ▸▸ *Recover the foot and hips first* ▸▸ *Recover the upper body* ▸▸ *Recover the arm.*

Errors Explored Through Resistance Lunging

What follows are descriptions of the most common alignment errors in the *lunge*. I recommend that you experiment with each error — meaning intentionally make the error and then correct it. By intentionally making an error of alignment you will better understand what the proper position feels like and the benefits of taking it.

Arm Alignment

While extending the arm, make sure the wrist, elbow joint, and the bones of the forearm stay in front of the body.

Explore how the *lunge* breaks down when you allow your elbow to stick out to the side, or your wrist to bend. (Be gentle with your wrist, do not attempt this with much force.)

Incorrect! Elbow should not be sticking out.

Incorrect! Broken alignment along the wrist.

Correct! Elbow and wrist are aligned with the body.

Shoulder Alignment

In a proper *lunge* you create a strong and straight line from the *sword-hand* to the back leg by aligning the shoulders so the *sword-side* leads. This creates both structural (bone) alignment and strong muscle chain alignment.[30] If you square your shoulders, the arm aligns with the shoulder, but the shoulder aligns with nothing, forcing your abs to resist twisting and thus do much more work to apply the strength of your legs.

Incorrect! Shoulder alignment is too square.

Correct! Body is strongly profiled to create powerful alignment from the target to the back foot.

Head Alignment

In a *lunge* you want to keep your head in behind your sword *hilt* and over your feet. If you tilt your head away from the sword, whether that is to your left or right or backward away from the sword, you will break your alignment with the ground.

Experiment with head position in this exercise to understand how it can affect your power and safety.

Incorrect! The head is tilted away from the lead shoulder.

Incorrect! The head and shoulders are leaning too far away from the lead shoulder.

Correct! The head is well aligned over the lead shoulder.

Foot Connection

The most powerful connection with the ground, for explosive muscle engagement, is through the whole foot.

Conduct a resistance *lunge* and experiment with pressing off of different parts of the foot: the ball of the foot, the heel, and the whole foot.

Though moving up to the ball of the foot is a great way to increase your reach at the end of your *lunge*, the initial push against the ground is much stronger when conducted with connection from the heel and ball of the foot together.

Correct! Push off the whole foot when you lunge.

Incorrect Order

Moving the hand, shoulders, and then hips provides you with protection behind the hilt of the sword as well as optimal alignment.

Attempt a resistance *lunge* where you leave the arm bent and attempt to push the shoulders or hips forward without a straight arm. Then attempt a *lunge* with the shoulders coming after the hips and feet.

The alignment of the bones of the arm allows the muscles of your arm to focus simply on maintaining straightness. Pushing your upper body forward connects the arm more directly with the lower body. You can then use the larger quadriceps and gluteus muscles to push into your partner.

Incorrect! An effective attack cannot be made with a bent arm.   *Incorrect! Right has sent their lower body ahead of their upper-body.*   *Correct! Always extend the arm and shoulders ahead of the lower body.*

Rising in the Lunge

When lunging correctly, it is important that you align your body behind the point of force. The step of the *lunge* is the most important transference of force and you want it to be directed toward the opponent, not up and over their head. The *lunge* should either stay level, or sink, not rise.

To explore the error, push upward with your back leg as you step in the *lunge*. This upward aspect will often look like a slight bob of your head and body as you *lunge* out.

With this error you will find it difficult to push your opponent with the full strength of your legs. You may also find that your sword arm may suddenly fly out in a random direction, as the straightness of your connection from the ground to your partner is broken.

Incorrect! Pushing upward with the back leg will cause your force to go off target.   *Correct! Push directly into your opponent. Sinking as you move forward.*

Chapter Four

In taking the just measure it is more useful that you go, as is often said, with a leaden sandal.

—Ridolfo Capoferro, *Gran Simulacro dell'Arte e dell'uso di Schermire*, 1610

MOVEMENT

How you move between the measures is perhaps the most essential skill in swordplay. Traditionally, students in fencing schools spent years in their practice of movement before doing anything serious with their swords. Though that rigour is not essential for most practitioners, fluid and stable mobility is essential to one's offence and defence. It forms the core of good fencing practice.

In this section you will learn how to move in and out of *measure* with both small and larger steps and how to coordinate these movements with those of your sword.

Advancing and Retreating Steps

The *advance* and *retreat* are the most essential steps in rapier fencing. Both are careful steps used to come to *measure*, and to make adjustments once you or your opponent are *in measure*. The distance covered by an *advance* or *retreat* is roughly half of one foot's length.

Advance

① Lift the lead toe.

② Place the heel where the toe was.

③ As the toe descends, move the back foot forward the same length to complete the step.

Lift the toe.

Place the front heel ahead one half foot-length.

Bring the back foot forward.

Retreat

① Push from the ball of your front foot.

② Reach your back foot one foot-length behind you.

③ Withdraw your front foot the same distance.

The goal is to be able to move quickly, easily, and in a manner that leaves you ready to defend or attack as soon as necessary.

When *advancing* and *retreating* be sure to:

- Keep the distance between your feet. Step with the front foot first when moving forward, the back foot when moving backward.
- Keep your weight on your back leg.
- Move smoothly and crisply.
- Pick up your feet.

Push from the front foot.

Reach with the back foot first.

Follow with the front foot.

Sideways Steps

Historical fencing is not a strictly linear game. It is important to know how to move right and left as well.

Step Right

① Push from the left foot to initiate the step.

② Place your right foot one foot-width to the right. Your stance will widen slightly as you do this and your weight will shift toward your right foot.

③ Step with the left foot the same distance to come back to the same stance width.

Push from the left foot.

Step with the right foot first.

Bring the left foot into line.

Step Left

① Push from the right foot to initiate the step.

② Place your left foot one foot-width to the left. Your stance will widen slightly as you do this and your weight will shift toward your left foot.

③ Step with the right foot the same distance to come back to the same stance width.

When stepping sideways it is important to keep the steps small so that you do not overly square your body (becoming a larger target).

Note that you are always stepping with the foot that is closest to the direction of movement (when stepping forward, the front foot, when stepping left, the left foot, etc), this keeps your base broad and stable and avoids crossing or gathering together of the feet.

Push with the right foot.

Step with the left foot first.

Bring the right foot into line.

Common Footwork Errors

Proper *advancing* and *retreating* should maintain weight over the back leg, a proper reclined angle to the body (in the *defensive posture*), and a smooth carriage where the head or hips do not bounce.

Weight Shifting

A common error is to place excessive weight onto the front foot when moving forward, thus exposing the flank or head to attack (when they are closer to your opponent), as well as the leg itself. Taking weight off the back leg also robs it of the ability to push you forward quickly when you attack.

Incorrect! Do not shift your weight forward when you step.

Correct! Note back leg, recline, and smooth movement.

Pigeon Walking

A variation on letting your weight come forward is letting the head come forward. This happens most commonly when retreating while in the *defensive posture*. Be sure to keep the head back while aligning the *off-side* breast, hip, and heel. If the head

Incorrect! Do not reach backward with your leg and push your head forward.

rocks forward while you reach back with your foot, it will be dangerously exposed to attack.

Bouncing

Be sure to keep your knees bent while moving. You want your head and body to glide forward at the same distance from the ground. It is common during an *advance* or *retreat* to overly straighten one of the legs, causing the body to become taller, and thus bounce. Bouncing is a waste of energy and gives your opponent greater warning when you are moving.

Incorrect! Do not allow your legs to straighten or to come up onto your toes.

Gather Stepping

Be sure to always maintain the distance between your feet in your stance, expanding as you step with the lead foot and returning to the proper distance between the feet as you complete the step.

Though there will be times when gathering is an advantageous technique, you do not want to do it unintentionally. *Advancing* and *retreating* steps should be kept small and precise. Don't rush.

Incorrect! Do not allow your feet to get closer together.

Drifting Toe/Knee

Keep your lead toe and knee directed toward your opponent and your rear knee over your rear toe.

The toe and knee act as a kind of pointer for your sword. Where they point the hips follow, and where the hips go so do the shoulders, hands, and finally your sword. In striking and defending it is essential for optimal strength and accuracy that your toe and knee stay *on-line*.

Toe and knee alignment is also an essential part of knee health. When you flex your leg, if your toe is pointing in one direction while your knee is heading in another, you will quickly do damage to the tendons at the joint.

Be sure to focus on groin and hip opening stretches when you conclude your workouts to help alleviate any muscle tension that contributes to this problem.

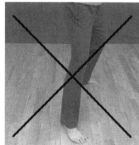 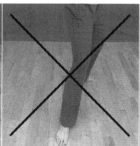 

Incorrect! Do not allow the toe to drift out of alignment from the knee.

Incorrect! Do not allow the knee to drift out of alignment from the hips or toe.

Correct! Keep the hips, knee, and toe in alignment along the line of direction.

Passing Steps

A *passing step* is a much larger step, where one foot passes the other. These steps are used to get out of measure quickly or approach an opponent who is a long way away.

The *passing step* is not used to move into your striking *measure*, and certainly not your opponent's, as the size of the step can leave you vulnerable to attack. You can use the *passing step* to move just outside of *measure* and then then use *advancing steps* to cover the last part of the distance.

The following instructions are written for someone holding their sword in their right hand with their right side leading.

A passing step is a step where one foot passes the other.

Passing Step Forward

① Begin in the *defensive posture*.

② Shift your weight onto your front/right foot, freeing your rear foot to step.

③ Lift the left/rear foot and cross it just ahead of the lead foot, maintaining your foot orientation.

④ Shift your weight onto your left foot (which is now in the lead).

⑤ Replace your right foot ahead of the left foot, approximately two foot-lengths apart.

Defensive posture.

Place the foot on the ground ahead of the lead/right foot.

Bring the lead/right foot through to return to the defensive posture.

Passing Step Back

① Begin in the *defensive posture*.

② Lift the lead/right foot and cross it behind your left/rear foot, maintaining your foot orientation.

③ Shift your weight onto your right foot (which is now in the rear). This will free your left foot to step.

④ Move your left foot behind your right foot to reform the proper *defensive posture*. Your feet should be approximately two foot-lengths apart.

Defensive posture.

Transfer your weight to the foot behind you.

Pass your left leg back. Return to the defensive posture.

Common Passing Step Errors

Over-shifting Your Weight

If you find at the end of a *passing step* forward you are needing to shift your weight back onto the rear foot you are most likely shifting too far forward at the end of the step. When concluding the forward *passing step* be sure to place your front foot down lightly maintaining the weight on your rear leg.

Incorrect! Do not let the weight shift over the front leg at the end of the pass. *Correct! Lightly place the foot so the defensive posture is maintained.*

Two ways you can help avoid this error:

① Practice the *passing step* in slow motion. Slowly shift the weight forward, pick up the rear foot and have it hang in the air for a long time as you bring it forward. Place it down gently and continue through with the front foot, slowly putting it in place in front of you. Doing a step slowly will help you develop the stabilizer muscles required to step fluidly and with balance. Don't be surprised if you find this more challenging than it sounds.

② Keep separation between your *passing steps* in practice. It is easy to let one *passing step* flow into another, which can lead to the weight shifting issue described. When you are first developing your *passing step*, be sure to allow for a pause between each full movement.

Turning the Hips

When making a *passing step*, you want to keep your *sword-side* leading throughout the step. Do not let your *off-side* come ahead of your *sword-side*.

You can maintain the orientation of your hips by also maintaining the orientation of your feet and shoulders. Leave the sword-arm strongly in front, your back foot pointing out toward your side, and your front foot pointing along the *line of direction* throughout the entire step.

Incorrect: Do not turn your hip and foot while you are passing. *Correct: Keep your hip and foot alignment while passing forward.*

Stepping Around the Lead Leg

When *passing* forward, many can find it difficult to navigate around the lead leg, especially when both feet rest on the *line of direction*.

Some will find it easier to increase the width of their stance slightly so that the heels are slightly *off-line* from one another. In this way you can pass more directly with the back foot, without feeling that the front foot is an obstacle.

Incorrect! Do not step directly in front of your lead foot.

Correct! Step slightly offset to allow the back leg to pass the front foot freely.

Simple Movement Drill

You can use this exercise to gain more fluidity and crispness in your steps.

① Start at one side of a room in the *defensive posture*. Make two *advancing steps* followed by one *retreating step*, and repeat, until you reach the opposite side.

② Then, make two *retreating steps* and one *advance*, repeating until you reach your starting position.

③ Change to the *offensive posture* and conduct the drill again.

Two advancing steps followed by one retreating step.

Two retreating steps followed by one advancing step.

Mirror Movement Drill

In this exercise you will have a partner test your movement and help you develop your ability to judge *misura*.

① Start facing across from your partner.

② Both you and your partner extend your swords into the *offensive posture* and approach one another until the point of your, or your partner's, sword touches the *hilt* of the other.

③ Stop at this place. You and your partner will return to the *defensive posture*. Observe the distance between you and your partner. Your job will be to stay at this same *measure* throughout the rest of the exercise.

④ Your partner will now step toward you or away from you using *advancing*, *retreating*, and *passing steps*. Your job is to maintain the same *measure*, established in step 3, using your own footwork.

Face your partner.

Establish misura.

⑤ Periodically your partner, as the leader, will check your *measure* by announcing "check." You both will then pause and extend your swords into the *offensive posture*. You can now observe how close to your starting measure you are and then adjust.

⑥ Switch leaders in the exercise on every third "check."

You do not need to match your partner's footwork exactly. The goal is to move with proper steps while maintaining *measure*. You may find, that depending on the height of your partner or the length of their legs, you may need to take more or fewer steps, or differently sized steps, to properly match them.

The follower has come too close and will need to adjust by making a retreat.

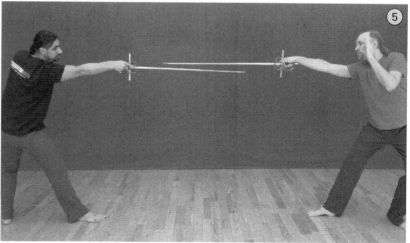

The follower is too far away and will need to adjust by making an advance.

Tactical: The Measure Game ▦

The simplest form of defence is distance. Now that you have attacking and movement skills under your belt you can take your first step toward sparring. This exercise is best done with protective equipment, at least a mask and gorget.

① Begin with you and your opponent *out of measure* from one another. You are in the *defensive posture*; your partner is also in the *defensive posture* but with their sword arm down and their point directed at the ground.

② Your job is to approach your partner and when you are in *measure*, attack with the appropriate *thrust* for that *measure*.

③ Your partner's job is to stay close enough that you believe you can strike them, but, then as you attack, to step back enough to not be struck.

④ You recover and lower your sword point to the floor.

⑤ Having avoided your *thrust*, your partner raises their point and you exchange roles.

⑥ Alternate striking, using only movement and distance to protect you, until someone has been struck. When someone is struck a point is scored and you reset by moving apart from one another.

The pace can increase as you get more comfortable in the exercise. You're playing a game of hit and not-get-hit. You're welcome to make a short range attack like a *lunge* and then extend it into a *passing lunge* to catch your partner off guard, or make a shorter attack than is needed, simply to trade turns while staying a bit farther from a long-limbed opponent.

As soon as you lower your sword you must receive your partner's attack. You cannot attack again until they have done so. It's also poor form to back your partner into a wall.

One of the best strategies is to retreat from an attack only as much as is necessary. Stay as close to their point as possible. Then, as they begin to lower their sword and retreat, follow immediately after with your counter-attack. To do this efficiently will require that you maintain good posture and form throughout, as well as attacking in good order: arm, shoulders, hips.

▦ Right is ready to attack ▶▶ Left has avoided the attack of Right ▶▶ It's Left's turn to attack ▶▶ Right did not move back enough.

Chapter Five

Anyone who in anger draws the sword he wears at his side, whether because of his own fury or some external provocation of word or deed, will raise his hand to form a guard.

—Camillo Agrippa, *Trattato di Scientia d'Arme*, 1556

GAINING THE SWORD

The art of fencing is first and foremost the art of defence. Your primary goal throughout any fight is to keep yourself safe. This is especially true when you are attempting to strike your opponent. A well-formed attack is not simply an offence; it is a defence that carries your weapon to its target.

As you make a *thrust* to your opponent you must first make sure that you have dealt with their weapon in some way that prevents it from being able to strike you, either simultaneously or pre-emptively. This could be done immediately before your attack, or more optimally, as a defence integrated into your attack.

The foundation for this idea of defence with offence are the techniques known as *finding* and *gaining* the sword.[31] In this section we'll explore how to employ these techniques as well as defining the *guards* of the rapier, *lines of attack*, and the beginnings of rapier tactics.

The Problem of the Point

Let's explicitly explore the problem you face when you want to attack an opponent who is threatening you with the point of their weapon.

① Place yourself at *misura larga* across from a partner.

② Have both of you take up the *defensive posture*. Have your partner direct their point at your chest.

③ Transition into the *offensive posture*, avoiding sword-to-sword contact with your partner's weapon. You will essentially be reaching over or around your partner's sword to do this.

④ Make a slow *lunge* to your partner's chest.

⑤ Have your partner keep their point *on-line* with your chest while you conduct your attack. Depending on relative arm or sword length you may be struck by your partner during, or at the end, of your attack. You may also find yourself very close to their point without having made contact with it.

This exercise probably feels rather uncomfortable. If you don't employ a technique to displace your partner's sword you're rushing toward certain death. Who cares if your point strikes its own target?

Left has let themselves get struck simultaneously with their own attack.

Finding

To *find* the sword is to place your opponent's weapon in a mechanically weak position where you can easily gain control of it.

Left has found the sword of Right.

Gaining

To *gain* the sword of the opponent is to fully negate its offensive capability and ideally negate its defensive capability as well. This makes you safe and leaves your opponent open to be struck.

Left has gained the sword of Right.

In this section you will learn how to properly *find* and *gain* your opponent's sword by using your sword and body's physical characteristics to best advantage.

Lines of Attack

Before you begin learning to *find* and *gain* the opponent's sword, a language is needed to describe where to strike and how.

Stand across from your partner with your weapon pointing towards their chest. Imagine a line extending from the point of your sword to your desired target. This imaginary line is the path that your sword must travel to strike the target with a *thrust*. This path is called the *line of attack*.

Left's sword can travel the line of attack into their opponent's shoulder.

There are infinite numbers of *lines of attack*, depending on your sword's position and your desired target. However to simplify things, these *lines* are divided into a few categories based on the position of your opponent's weapon.

Provided you are facing an opponent who is holding their sword in their right hand, all of the targets to the right of their sword (from your perspective) are on the *inside line*. All of the targets to the left of their sword (from your perspective) are on the *outside line*. Targets above the *hilt* of the sword are on the *high line*. Targets below are on the *low line*.

So if you are striking a target that is to right of their sword and above their *hilt*, you are striking them on the "high, inside line". If you are striking below, and to the left of their hilt, your target is on a "low, outside line".

Be mindful that their sword's position is what determines the *line* of the target. You may strike twice to an opponent's breast pocket. If the first time their sword is to the left of yours then the target is on the *inside*. If, the second time, they have moved their sword so it is to the right of yours you are striking on their *outside*.

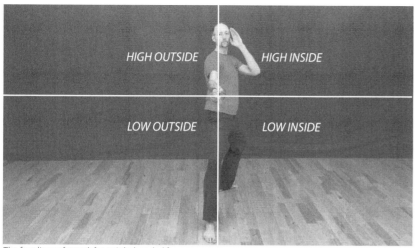

The four lines of attack for a right handed fencer.

The four lines of attack for a left handed fencer.

Crossing Swords

If you walk toward a partner, while both your swords are on-line, somewhere around *misura larghissima* your points will pass one another. At this point your swords are "crossed", regardless of whether or not they are in-contact with each other. The crossing forms an "X" when viewed from the side.

The "X" is the crossing.

If you cross swords with your opponent, with your sword to the right of theirs, they are on **your** *inside line* and you are also on **their** *inside line*.

Now, if your opponent is holding their sword in their left hand while you are holding your sword in your right—things change. If you cross with their sword to your left they are still on **your** *inside line* but you are on **their** *outside line*.

Many exercises will call on you to place your opponent's sword in a particular relationship to your own, for example: "find your opponent's sword on your inside;" to a right-hander this would mean to have their sword to the left of yours, to a left-hander it would mean the opposite (regardless in which hand your opponent is holding their sword).

If high or low are not specified the default placement is high. You will also encounter requests to strike your opponent in a particular *line*, in which case it is irrelevant which hand you are holding your sword in. What is relevant is on which side of your opponent's sword your blade is crossing when you strike.

Right has struck Left in the chest on their high, outside line.

The Three Advantages

To learn how to *find* and *gain* in a given *line*, you must understand how to successfully push the opponent's sword away while keeping yours on-line. To do this you must understand three principles of blade interaction called the *three advantages*.

True Edge

Turning the *true edge* of your sword toward your opponent's weapon creates mechanical strength through orientation of your wrist and arm, structural strength by engaging the more rigid edge, and deflection through engaging the width of the blade. This could be expressed as a simple rule: "always turn your knuckles toward your opponent's sword."

Right has turned his true edge toward his partner's sword.

Leverage

The sword and hand form a lever. The lever of the sword rests on a fulcrum which is typically the finger looped under the *ricasso*. As the pressure on the weapon's *debole* increases, the force exerted on this fulcrum finger will become pronounced as the sword fighter attempts to prevent the deviation of

Left has the advantage of leverage.

the weapon. Being able to apply the *forte* of your sword against the *debole* of your opponent's sword is an essential part of controlling their weapon.

Crossing

This advantage, sometimes expressed as the rule "always be on top", is where you place the blade of your sword over the blade of the opponent. This creates an environment where the *debole* of the opponent's sword is more inclined to slide down into your *forte* and thus increase your leverage.

Right has the advantage of crossing.

The Advantage of the True Edge

The following exercises will help you understand how orienting the *true edge* (the edge of the sword that aligns with your knuckles) adds to the sword's structural strength while aligning your body's mechanical strength, and how the width of the blade and the orientation of your hand causes the opponent's sword to be deflected away from your body. Then you will learn four hand and arm positions, the *guards*, that codify this edge placement.

Exercise: Rigidity and Mechanical Alignment

In this exercise you will explore how the rigidity of the edge, verses the flexibility of the flat of your blade, allows you to more easily apply force to your opponent's weapon.

① Place yourself across from a partner in the defensive posture. Cross swords, on the inside line, about 10 inches from the points. Make sure that you are both crossing at the same place on the blade and that the flats of your blades are touching.

② Push against each other's swords. Essentially try to push the sword of your partner out of the way, while they try to do the same. Observe what happens to the blades and the feeling in your hand and arm.

③ Turn your *true edge* to your partner's sword by turning your hand palm-up. Keep your swords crossing in the same place and remain in contact with the flat of your partner's blade. Observe how your partner's blade flexes when you are pushing and yours does not. Also note how much more easily you can push your partner's blade aside.

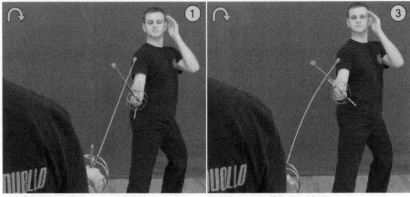

Both flats are touching.   Right has turned his true edge.

④ Switch roles. Note the change in blade flexion and ability to apply strength.

A sword blade's lenticular shape (meaning it is wide and thin) makes it structurally stronger (less able to flex) along the axis of its edge. Thus, when your sword's edge is turned in, more force is communicated through your weapon. Turning the *true edge* also aligns the edge, your hand, and arm, so you can more effectively push into your opponent's sword. If you were to use your *false edge* (the edge opposite the *true edge*) your blade would not flex, but you would not be able to push. You would instead be pulling, which is a weaker mechanical action.

Exercise: Deflection

① Place yourself across from a partner standing in the *defensive posture*.

② Take the *offensive posture* and cross swords on your *high outside* at the *mezza spada* (middle of your blades). Let the swords gently rest against each other, flat against flat. Your partner's sword should be pointed at your face, just above the *hilt* of your sword.

③ Turn your *true edge* towards your partner's blade by turning your hand palm-down. Maintain contact with their blade and continue to keep your own point oriented toward your partner. As you turn your edge, your partner's sword will be pushed farther to your *outside* and away from its target.

Right is in the offensive posture.   *Right has turned his true edge to the outside.*

This occurs for two reasons:

1. Turning the edge makes your blade "wider", and thus creates more deflection.
2. When you hold the sword it sits more to one side of your hand (toward the knuckles) than the other (toward your thumb). The off-centre position of the sword then increases the deflection of the edge on the knuckle side.

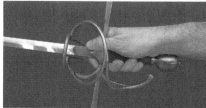 

Note the pommel's position to the inside of the wrist. If you turn your true edge away from their sword, you'll notice the deflection does not occur.   *Incorrect! Left has turned their true edge away from their partner's sword. Right's sword thus remains on-line and threatening.*

Exercise: Following the Sword

By keeping your *true edge* toward your opponent's sword you guard your body from their point. In this exercise we will explore this idea and begin to understand proper hand position for defence.

① Place yourself across from a partner standing in the *defensive posture*.

② Take the *offensive posture* and cross swords on your *high inside*.

③ Turn your *true edge* so it points directly toward your partner's sword on your *inside*.

④ Have your partner slowly move their sword from one side of your blade to the other by making a circle underneath it (*inside* to *outside*). It will start by moving below yours and you will follow it so your *true edge* points toward the floor.

True edge inside.   *True edge down.*

⑤ Then to your *outside*.

⑥ Then toward the ceiling.

True edge outside.   *True edge up.*

⑦ Follow their sword all the way back in the opposite direction until you are again palm-up on the inside with your true edge oriented to your inside.

Hand Positions

Codified originally by engineer and fencer Camillo Agrippa in his 1553 treatise, the four hand positions represent the four most optimal placements of the sword for defence and offence.[32]

Hand positions relate both to the orientation of the edge and to the position of the hand in front of the body: in front of your flank, right shoulder, head, etc.

You can imagine these positions as points on a clock, where your brow is the 12, and your flank (at the bottom of your ribcage) is the 6. The 3 and 9 positions are then occupied by your right and left shoulders.

In each position the *true edge* and *knuckle-bow* are oriented toward the outside of the clock.

The hand positions are the quarter hours of a clock. Seen from the fencer's perspective.

I. Prima (12 o'clock – true edge up)

- Fully extend your arm and place the sword at the height of your head over your sword shoulder with your fingernails oriented toward your *outside*.
- The *knuckle-bow* and *true edge* orient toward the ceiling.
- Keep the point directed at the opponent with the blade parallel with the floor.
- Place your thumb beneath the grip to support the blade.

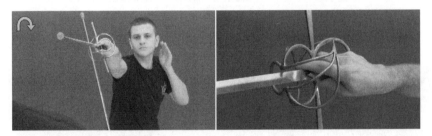

II. Seconda (3 o'clock – true edge outside)

- Lower your sword and extend it in front of your sword shoulder with your fingernails oriented toward the floor.
- The *true edge* is oriented to your *outside* (your right, if your sword is in your right hand).
- The pommel rests beneath your palm or wrist.

III. Terza (6 o'clock – true edge down)

- Lower your hand to the height of your waist with your hand palm-down with your fingernails oriented toward the *inside*.
- Bend your elbow so your forearm is parallel with the floor.
- The handle or pommel resting against the heel of your hand.
- Keep the point of your elbow oriented toward the floor.

IV. Quarta (9 o'clock – true edge inside)

- Fully extend the arm and place the hilt in front of your *off-side* shoulder with your fingernails oriented toward the ceiling.
- Your *true edge* is oriented to your *inside* (your left, if your sword is in your right hand).
- A straight line is formed from your *off-side shoulder*, to your hand, to the point of your sword, then to your target.

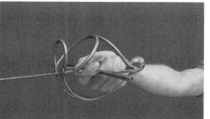

Why Is It Called Prima?

Prima, which is the Italian word for "first", is the first position your sword easily finds when drawn from a scabbard. To explore this, try this sword-drawing exercise:

① Stand with both feet together, with your *sword-side* shoulder oriented toward your opponent.

② Grip the top of your scabbard in your *off-hand*. (If you do not have a scabbard simply grip your sword blade ahead of the *hilt*, as if it were in a scabbard).

③ Reach across your body with your *sword-hand* and place it on the handle of your rapier, in a proper grip with your finger extended over the *ricasso*.

④ Push your scabbard backward with your *off-hand* while drawing your sword with your *sword-hand*. The action will describe a diagonal arc from your *off-side* hip out into *prima* on your *sword-side*. Your knuckles and *true edge* will keep their same orientation throughout the entire motion.

⑤ Step back with your *sword-side* foot, while drawing the sword, allowing your shoulders to turn away from the scabbard.

⑥ Finish the turn of the body bringing you fully in to *prima* with your *off-side* foot in the front. *Prima* not only frees the sword—it presents an immediate threat to your opponent.

⑦ You can now step forward or back and take one of the *guards* we're about to see.

Push down the scabbard.   *Turn the shoulders.*   *Step back into prima.*

Guards

A *guard* (in Italian *guardia*) is the combination of a hand position with a body posture. They are so named because their primary goal, whether defending or threatening, is to guard your body from attack. The *guards* follow the same naming convention as the hand positions. Each hand position could be combined with the *defensive posture* (hand low by the flank) or the *offensive posture* (with the hand high by the face and the upper body reaching forward). There are four default combinations:

Prima Guardia

The *guard* of *prima* combines the hand position of *prima* with the *offensive posture*.

- The sword is extended in front of the *sword-shoulder* with the *hilt* at brow height.
- The *off-side shoulder* stays back and in-line with the *hilt*, profiling the body behind the weapon.

It can be difficult with *prima* to not feel compelled to contort the torso to place the arm and hand in the correct position. Use the exercise in the section on posture to find the correct *offensive posture* with your sword palm-down (*seconda*), then keep the body firmly in place and move only the arm and hand into the *prima* position. You will also find placing your thumb beneath the grip, as shown in the hand position section, will make the *guard* easier to form and maintain.

Prima in profile.

Incorrect! Keep the hips under the shoulders and the arm and head aligned to the line of direction.

Prima facing the camera.

Seconda Guardia

The *guard* of *seconda* combines the hand position of *seconda* with the *offensive posture.*

- The sword is extended in front of the *sword-shoulder.*
- The body is lowered behind the sword, hiding as much of the upper chest as possible behind the protection of the *hilt* and *forte.*
- The head is alongside the sword-arm, with your eyes looking through, or just above the rings of the *hilt*, and down the length of the blade.
- The *off-side shoulder* stays behind your *hilt*, as much as possible.
- The wrist joint should be straight, with the back of the hand forming a flush line with the back of the arm.

Be sure to keep your hips underneath your shoulders. It's easy, when forming *seconda*, to allow your buttocks to stick out on your *sword-side*. Keep the shoulders relaxed and the neck elongated as you look down your rapier. Avoid hunching your shoulders or scrunching your head down.

Seconda in profile.

Incorrect! Keep the hips tucked in, the sword-arm at shoulder height, and the arm and shoulders along the line of direction.

Seconda facing the camera.

Terza Guardia

The *guard* of *terza* is the only *guard* that is by default formed with the *defensive posture*.

- The sword is held ahead of the sword shoulder, at the height of the lower ribs, to the outside of the *sword-side* knee.
- Hold the forearm parallel with the ground.
- Keep one hand-span of distance between your sword elbow and your side to allow for movement of the sword.
- Keep your sword elbow tucked in and pointing toward the ground, so it does not point toward your outside.

This is the most protective of the *guards* and is used to cautiously approach *measure* and to wait for the opponent. Here, with the head withdrawn and the sword central to the body, you can easily move to any of the other *guards*.

Terza in profile.

Incorrect! Shoulders are square to the line of direction, sword arm is bent to the side.

Correct: Keep the shoulders profiled and along the line of direction, the hilt of the sword on the line of direction and the elbow of the sword-arm tucked in.

Quarta Guardia

The *guard* of *quarta* combines the hand position of *quarta* with the *offensive posture*.

- The sword is extended in front of the *off-side* shoulder.
- The body is lowered behind the sword, hiding as much of the upper chest as possible behind the protection of the *hilt* and *forte*.
- The head is to the outside of the *hilt* with your eyes looking down the *false edge* of the blade.
- The body maintains the same degree of profile as the other *guards*.
- The arm is straight so that your elbow and the underside of your arm are protected by the *hilt*.

Quarta can protect both high and low on the *inside line*. The *hilt* can be raised, as needed, up to the same height as *prima*.

Practice

Practice moving between the *guards* in front of a mirror or an observant partner. The goal is to move crisply through each position while moving only the parts of the body essential to change *guards*. Keep in mind that *prima*, *seconda*, and *quarta* share the same body position, so nothing needs to move other than the arm and hand when you are transitioning between them.

Quarta in profile.

Incorrect! Keep the hips under the shoulders and the hilt in line with the off-side shoulder.

Quarta facing the camera.

The Advantage of Leverage

Your sword is a lever that both you and your opponent can use.

The functioning of your sword as a lever is both its greatest strength and its greatest weakness. Using your handle as a lever (above right) allows you to move your point very quickly. However, your opponent can also use your blade as a lever, to displace your point (below right). Like with any lever, the longer it is (or the farther you are from the fulcrum) the stronger you will be.

When swords come into contact for a prolonged period, or simply for an instant, it becomes a lever vs lever battle. The following exercise will help you understand how this lever-on-lever contact plays out in a sword fight and how to best position your weapon to maximize leverage in your favor.

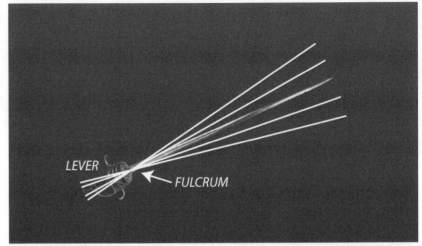

Your sword as your lever

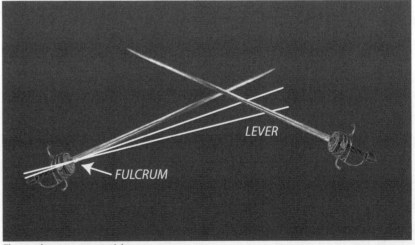

The sword as your opponent's lever

Exercise: Winning Leverage

The sword blade is divided into two halves: 1. The *debole* (English: weak), the half closest to the point. 2. The *forte* (English: strong), the half closest to the hilt. The dividing point of these halves is called the *mezza spada* (English: middle sword).

① Stand with your partner, in *terza*, your swords crossed at the *mezza spada* on the *high inside line*.

② Have your partner place the *debole* of their sword into the *forte* of yours.

③ Have a pushing battle with both of you attempting to push the other's sword right and left. Be sure to keep the relationship of *debole* on *forte* throughout. Note that you are significantly more able to push your partner's sword.

④ Have your partner place two hands onto their handle and attempt to double their strength. You should continue to be able to win the pushing battle, provided you maintain the position of your *forte* on their *debole*.

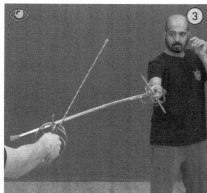

Left has the advantage of leverage.   *Right is attempting to resist using two hands.*

⑤ Switch roles. Place your *debole* into your partner's *forte* and repeat the steps. See how the change of leverage changes who is able to win the battle.

Exercise: Using Guards to Win Leverage

① Stand again with your partner, in *terza*, your swords crossed at the *mezza spada* on the *high inside line*.

② Now extend into *quarta* (the correct guard for applying the *advantage of true edge*) and place your *forte* against their *debole*. Keep your point directed at their face.

③ Play the pushing game as before. Note that as long as you maintain the same strong-on-weak relationship, your partner cannot push your point away from its target, and your own face and upper body are protected.

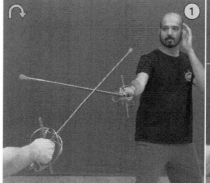

Equal crossing in the mezza spada.   *Right has gained leverage by going to quarta.*

Though differences in physical strength between the partners can make a difference in this exercise, when you are optimally positioned against your partner's sword, even the strongest partner will be unable to overcome you. This is one of the beautiful things about swordplay: when done well, victory is about position and strategy, not simply brawn and audacity.

The Advantage of Crossing

This advantage is the most powerful of the *three advantages*. You get this *advantage* by directing your point over your opponent's sword. This does two things:

1. You create a guiding path for your opponent's sword that causes their point (and thus their *debole*) to slide down into your *forte*, increasing your leverage.

2. You put gravity on your side (they're lifting away from it, you're moving with it). It also puts you in the mechanically superior position of pushing down while they're in the weaker position of lifting up.

In conclusion, always lead with the point. When you cross swords, by directing your point first towards a target that is across your opponent's sword, you naturally create a slope which guides the opposing force into your *forte*. When responding to an opposing force use your point to oppose it, instead of attempting to push with your *hilt*. This will cause the opponent's point to be channeled into your *hilt* more effectively.

The following exercises will show you several different ways this *advantage* can be applied.

Exercise: Being On Top

① Have both you and your partner place yourselves in *terza*, in the *offensive posture*, with your blades parallel to the floor.

② Approach your partner. Allow your blade to pass on the *outside* of theirs.

③ Direct your point so it crosses over top of your partner's blade on the *outside* (pointing toward their chest or *off-side* shoulder), while maintaining its overall position parallel to the floor.

④ Have your partner attempt to push your sword to the right (your left) by lifting their point and pushing. This is done with their arm straight by directing from the wrist or shoulder.

⑤ Hold your sword firmly over theirs. Keep your point down so the blade stays parallel with the floor and your point stays directed at its target. The best way to resist your partner's attempt to push you is to keep your point on target. Do not attempt to stop them by pushing with your *forte* or hand.

⑥ Continue moving your point towards your partner while maintaining the crossing. Keep your face and torso hidden behind the *hilt*. You will see that your partner's point will slide down into your *hilt* and be deflected aside while your point stays *on-line* until you have struck.

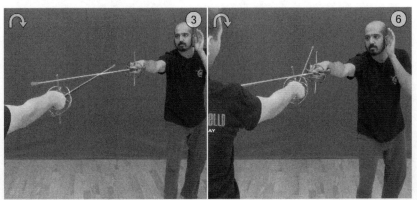

Right is crossed over Left's sword.

Right maintains their position and deflects Left's sword as they strike.

Exercise: Crossing a Defensive Sword

The power of crossing can also be seen when you and your partner are in the *defensive posture* with the *hilts* low and the points high.

① Cross swords with your partner in *terza* on the inside at the *mezza spada*. Have an equal position of leverage, with your *hilts* in front of your flanks and your points at the height of the shoulder.

② Attempt to cross your point over your partner's sword, while they attempt to do the same. Your swords should stay roughly in the same place while you both feel the pressure of the other's resistance.

③ Stop applying pressure. Your partner will now allow you to direct your point over their sword.

④ Point toward your partner's sword shoulder (your *off-side*) so your blade forms an angle overtop of their sword.

⑤ Have your partner push again on your blade without attempting to change their leverage position.

⑥ Slowly extend your point toward your opponent's body by stepping forward or reaching forward with your shoulders. Do not raise your *hilt* or lower your point. Keep your *hilt* low and your tip high, even when extending your shoulders forward.

The pressure into your sword, combined with the crossing you are creating overtop, should cause your partner's point to drop into your *forte*, and make it difficult to direct it back into your *debole*.

Fencers are pushing in a neutral (even) crossing.   *Left's point has slid down into Right's forte.*

Exercise: Using a Straight Line to Defeat an Oblique Line

In the previous two exercises the opponent's weapon was directed at the centre of your body. This required that you direct your point over their sword by pointing it right or left, thus forming an oblique line in the horizontal axis. If your partner's sword is itself forming an oblique line, then to cross it you simply need to keep your sword straight (note: you can still have a vertical angle to your sword, i.e. *hilt* low, point high).

① Have your partner stand in *seconda* with their blade parallel with the floor and their point angled strongly to the *inside*. This will put their *hilt* in front of their *sword-side* shoulder and their point in front of their *off-side* shoulder.

② Take *terza*, with your *hilt* in front of your flank and your point at the height of your partner's throat.

③ Without deviating your position, walk slowly towards your partner. Have your blade meet theirs at the *mezza spada*. Your sword will cross over their angled sword as you move toward your target.

④ Have your partner attempt to bring their point *on-line* or deflect your point as you press against their sword. Continue to your target without deviation. Affirm your position simply by pushing down with your point and pressing it firmly toward its target. Your partner will find your sword impossible to deflect without significant repositioning of their sword in relation to yours.

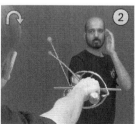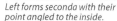

Left forms seconda with their point angled to the inside.   *Right crosses on the outside with a straight line and walks forward.*   *Left is unable to push Right away.*

Gaining the Sword – Approaching ▣

When you put the *three advantages* together in an *offensive guard* you have *gained* the opponent's sword. *Gaining* a sword is what makes it possible for you to strike an opponent with safety.

① Have your partner stand, *out of measure*, in *terza* with their point directed at your face.

② Approach until you arrive at *misura larga*, with their sword *outside* of yours.

③ Transition into *seconda guardia* and use it to gain all *three advantages* and push your partner's point aside.

- Direct your point toward the centre of your partner's upper chest (*crossing*).

- Extend your arm and place your *hilt* against your partner's *debole* (*leverage*).

- Push your shoulders forward and turn your arm and hand into *seconda* (*true edge*). This action should push the opponent's point up and to your *outside*, leaving you safe to strike.

- **You have now *gained* the opponent's sword.** Ensure that you are in a proper *offensive posture* and that your weight is still carried over your rear leg.

Right has gained the sword of Left on the outside.   *Viewed from the opposite perspective.*

④ From the *gaining* position, propel yourself into a *lunge* and strike your partner in the chest. Be sure to keep yourself extended in *seconda* as you do so. Your partner's sword should be directed safely past your body as you strike.

Right strikes with a lunge.   *Viewed from the opposite perspective.*

⑤ Recover your *lunge* into *seconda*. You are again in the *gaining* position.

⑥ Now retreat out of *measure*. Continue to protect yourself with your *hilt* and the *three advantages* for as long as possible.

▣   Right approaches ▸▸   Right arrives at misura larga ▸▸   Right gains Left's sword ▸▸   Right strikes with a lunge.

Exercise: Gaining the Sword on the Inside

Now let's try the same exercise on the *inside line* using *quarta* to *gain* the sword.

① Begin *out of measure*.

② Approach until you arrive at *misura larga*, with your partner's sword to your *inside*.

③ Transition into *quarta* and use it to gain all three *advantages* and push your partner's sword aside.

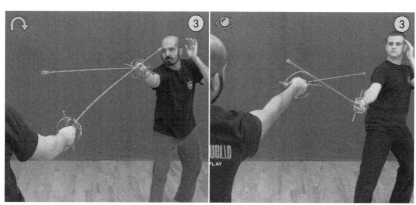

Right gains the sword of Left on the inside.   *Viewed from the opposite perspective.*

④ Strike with a *lunge* maintaining the *advantages*.

⑤ Recover to *quarta*.

⑥ Retreat from *measure*.

During the *gaining* exercises, you can have your partner give you light resistance to help you test your position. The best way to provide resistance is to attempt to direct your point, through your partner's sword, at their chest.

Finding the Sword

You've learned how to *gain* your opponent's sword, pushing it aside so that it cannot strike and setting your weapon up to deliver a thrust. However, what's to stop them from doing the same? Upon arriving at *misura larga*, provided all things are equal, it's going to be a race to see who can get into an offensive *guard* and gain the *advantages* first. You don't want to trust your safety to games of speed and chance.

If you are going to win the race to *gain* the sword, every time, you need to have a head start. That head start is known as *finding the sword*.

Left has found a portion of each advantage while approaching in terza.

Finding is essentially a defensive form of *gaining*, generally done in *terza*. When you *find* you acquire a portion of each of the *three advantages* sufficient to make it difficult for your opponent to *gain* in that same *line*. If, at this point, your opponent attempts to *gain* your sword you already have a portion of *crossing*, *leverage*, and *true edge*, so you are more sure to *gain* first.

Exercise: Finding and Gaining on the Outside 🎞

The process of *finding* your partner's sword, and beginning to acquire the *three advantages*, starts before the swords cross.

① Start *out of measure* from your partner with both of you in *terza* with your points directed at your partners' face.

② Slowly approach *misura larga*, one careful step at a time. Place your partner's sword on your *outside*.

③ Aim your sword toward your opponent's *off-side* shoulder before your sword points pass. This will set you up to place your opponent's sword under yours and give you the *advantage of crossing*. Direct the crossing from your elbow. Avoid breaking the wrist.

④ Turn your *true edge* so that it is oriented halfway between terza and seconda. Keep your hilt low. As your points pass one another you will have the *advantage of crossing* and a partial *advantage of edge*.

⑤ Cross your partner's sword and stay in their *debole*, approximately one hand-span from their point.

⑥ Elevate your point using your wrist and fingers to stay at the same place in their *debole*. Apply a downward pressure to force their sword under yours and into your *mezza spada*. This will give you the *advantage of leverage*. You should now have arrived at *misura larga* and have all *three advantages*. **You have *found* your partner's sword.**

⑦ Push your sword and upper body forward to fully *gain* your partner's sword in *seconda*. Be sure to have your *hilt* in front of your *sword-shoulder*. Direct your point toward your partner's centreline, at their chest or face. The process of *gaining* should:

- Place their *debole* firmly against your *forte* or *hilt* (depending on how close you are).
- Fully apply your *true edge* to deflect their sword *off-line*.
- Push your partner's point sufficiently *off-line* in a way that allows you to aim straight to your target while maintaining the *advantage of crossing*.

⑧ Conduct your *thrust* with a *lunge*. Maintain all of the *advantages*.

⑨ Recover the *lunge* to *seconda* (you are still in a *gaining* position).

⑩ Return to *terza*, *finding* their sword as you do so.

⑪ Retreat from *measure*. Maintain as much of the *three advantages* as possible as you withdraw.

Right finds Left's sword on the outside.   Viewed from the opposite perspective.

Right approaches ▸▸   Right find's Left's sword on the outside ▸▸   Right gains in seconda ▸▸   Right strikes with a lunge ▸▸   Right recovers to seconda.

Exercise: Finding and Gaining on the Inside ▦

① Start *out of measure* from your partner with both of you in *terza* with your points directed at your partners' face.

② Slowly approach *misura larga*, one careful step at a time. Place your partner's sword on your *inside*.

③ Aim your sword at your partner's *sword-shoulder* before your sword points pass. This will set you up to place your partner's sword under yours and give you the *advantage of crossing*. Direct the crossing from your wrist. Be sure to keep your *hilt* in front of your *sword-side* knee. Avoid allowing your hand to drift toward your *inside*, this would make it harder to create and maintain the *advantage of crossing*.

④ Turn your *true edge* so that it is oriented halfway between *terza* and *quarta*. Keep your *hilt* low. As your points pass one another you will have the *advantage of crossing* and a partial *advantage of true edge*.

⑤ Cross your partner's sword and stay in their *debole*, approximately one hand-span from their point.

⑥ Elevate your point using your wrist and fingers to stay at the same place in their *debole*. Apply a downward pressure to force their sword under yours and into your *mezza spada*. This will give you the *advantage of leverage*. You should now have arrived at *misura larga* and have all *three advantages*. **You have *found* your partner's sword.**

⑦ Push your sword and upper body forward to fully *gain* the sword in *quarta*. Be sure your *hilt* is in front of your *off-side* shoulder. Direct your point toward their chest, face, or lead shoulder. The process of *gaining* should:

- Place their *debole* firmly against your *forte* or *hilt* (depending on how close you are).
- Fully apply your *true edge* to deflect their sword *off-line*.
- Push your partner's point sufficiently *off-line* in a way that allows you to aim straight to your target while maintaining the *advantage of crossing* (more on this later).

⑧ Conduct your *thrust* with a *lunge*. Maintain all of the *advantages*.

⑨ Recover the *lunge* to *quarta* (you are still in a *gaining* position).

⑩ Return to *terza*, *finding* their sword as you do so.

⑪ Retreat from *measure*. Maintain as much of the *three advantages* as possible as you withdraw.

Right has found the sword of Left on the inside.   Viewed from the opposite perspective.

Right approaches ▸▸   Right finds Left's sword on the inside ▸▸   Right gains on their inside ▸▸   Right strikes with a lunge ▸▸   Right recovers to quarta.

Straight Lines and Oblique Lines

Crossing is the most powerful of the *three advantages* because it channels an opposing force into your *hilt*, thus maximizing your leverage. It is vital that you acquire and maintain it throughout the process of *finding* and *gaining* to stay safe while you strike your opponent. This sometimes requires that the way you cross change while you approach.

Crossing a Straight Line

If your opponent presents you with a straight line you will first cross it with an oblique line as you *find* them. Then as you *gain*, you will force their sword into an oblique line with your *hilt* and thus will cross them with a straight line.

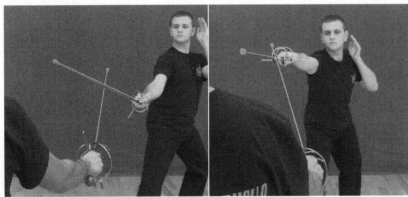

Right has used an oblique line to find a straight line.

Right has forced a straight line into an oblique line.

The oblique line formed with *finding* is a *defensive crossing* because your alignment with your target is not as direct but your safety is more assured. The straight line formed when *gaining* is an *offensive crossing* because the crossing is created while directing the point in a straight line to its target.

You may find, when making a *defensive crossing*, that your point must be *off-line* to sufficiently cross, i.e., not directed at a target. This is ok. The point can be redirected to a target very quickly. Keep it within the silhouette of your opponent's body so that it can act defensively while still presenting a threat.

Right has kept their point threatening to their opponent.

Right has put their point too far off-line to be threatening.

Crossing an Oblique Line

If your opponent presents you with an oblique line, then you can use an *offensive crossing* throughout your approach. You will thus *find* and *gain* with a straight line.

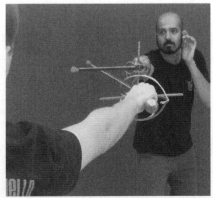

Right finds an oblique line with a straight line.

Winning the Gaining Race

To understand how advantageous it is to *find*, and how dangerous it is to be *found*, let's have a race with your partner.

① Start *out of measure* from your partner with both of you in *terza*.

② Approach your partner, as before, and *find* their sword on your *inside* at *misura larga*.
You have now *found* their sword, and they have not *found* yours.

③ Both of you to attempt (at the same speed) to *gain* the sword of the other.

④ Wait for your partner to begin *gaining*, then counter them by using the *advantages* you have already gained to keep control and win the race. It is essential that you keep the *advantage of crossing* throughout. Keep their sword beneath yours by pressing slightly downward with your point as you extend into *quarta*.

⑤ Repeat this exercise with you and your partner in the opposite roles. In this way you will understand both the advantage of *finding* and the disadvantage of being *found*.

This is a useful exercise not only for illustrating this point but also for building your ability to *gain* when you're under pressure. It is worth practicing it on the *inside* and *outside*.

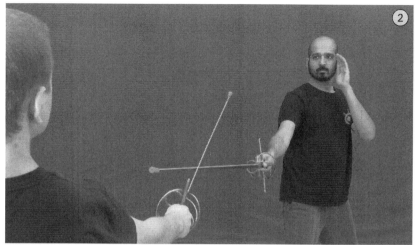

Left has found the sword of Right.

Right has found Left's sword on their inside.

Right and Left both attempt to gain at the same time. Right wins.

Left and Right attempt to gain at the same time. Left wins.

Open, Closed, and Constrained Lines

Now that you understand how to *find* and *gain* a sword, we can explore a final idea about *lines*. As you have experienced, not all *lines of attack* are available for striking. *Lines* have three states depending on the position of your opponent's sword in relation to yours:

An **open line** is a *line of attack* that leads directly to your target and has no influences applied over it by your opponent. The *line* has not been *found* or *gained*. As you travel this *line*, you may acquire one or all of the *advantages* over the opponent's sword.

A **constrained line** is a *line of attack* that is not *closed* but has been compromised because the opposing sword fighter has *found* it by applying a small part of each of the *three advantages*.

A **closed line** is a *line of attack* that cannot be followed because a weapon or other defensive object has gotten in its way. *Lines* are commonly *closed* through *gaining*, where the *three advantages* are fully acquired and applied against a sword.

Using an understanding of *finding* and *gaining*, you can choose to attack on *lines* that are *open* and where you have the best chance of *constraining* (*finding*) and *closing* (*gaining*) the *line* to your opponent.

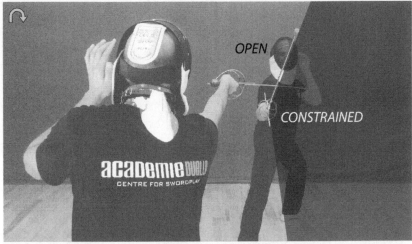

Right has constrained the inside line by finding it. The outside line is open.

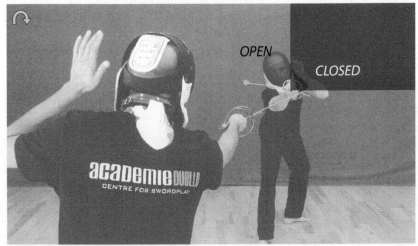

Right has closed the high inside line by gaining it.

CONSTRAINED

OPEN

Right has constrained the outside line by finding it. The inside line is open.

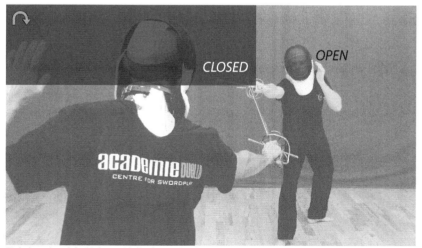

CLOSED

OPEN

Right has closed the high outside line by gaining it.

Tactical: Gaining Choice Drill

   In this exercise your partner will present you with random opportunities to *find*, *gain*, and strike on the *inside* and *outside*. By switching between skills at random your will increase your ability to choose the right skill. This exercise is best done with protective equipment (mask and gorget minimum).

① Begin *out of measure* from your partner. Both of you in *terza*, points high.

② Your partner will *invite* you to *find* them on their *inside* by pointing slightly toward their *outside* OR to *find* them on their *outside* by pointing slightly toward their *inside*. By doing this it makes it slightly easier to *find* the *advantage of crossing* on one side or the other (more on this later).

③ Approach and *find*, *gain*, and strike in the appropriate *line*.

④ Your partner will test your position by either pushing on your sword with their point or attempting to extend their sword to strike you.

⑤ After you have struck or failed to strike, recover and move *out of measure*. Your partner will then *invite* you again. Repeat 5 times and then switch roles.

   You could make this drill slightly more challenging by moving backward and forward with your partner (like the mirror movement drill) in between each invitation. In this way you will have to practice managing *measure* and making approaches.

Right has made an invitation on their outside.

Right has made an invitation on their inside.

Tactical: The Measure Game II

In this version of the measure game (see the previous section on movement for the original), your goal is to *gain* your partner's sword and strike at the appropriate *measure*.

① Begin with you and your partner *out of measure* from one another. You will both be in *terza*.

② Your job is to approach your partner, *find* their sword and, when you are at the appropriate *measure*, *gain* and strike.

③ Your partner's job is to stay close enough that you believe you can strike them, but, then as you attack, to step back enough to not be struck.

④ After having attacked you switch roles with your partner. They should immediately *find* your sword (on the *inside* or *outside*) and attempt to come into your *measure* and strike.

⑤ Continue alternating until someone is struck. Then reset.

You can test your partner's *gaining* of your sword by attempting to bring your point *on-line* as they attack (see Winning the Gaining Race, earlier in this chapter). If they run onto your point they'll know to do a better job of *gaining* next time.

Right attacks and Left avoids.

Left returns an attack. Right is struck because he did not move back in time.

Chapter Six

> *To one who is without this understanding & knowledge no*
> *guard has value. This is what the guards are.*
> —Nicoletto Giganti, *Scola overo Teatro*, 1606

APPROACHING DIFFERENT GUARDS

There are many different factors that will affect how you need to *find* and *gain* an opponent's sword. If they are holding it higher or lower or further to the *inside* or *outside*, each variation requires that you acquire the advantages in a slightly different fashion.

In this section we will explore the best *lines* of approach against various *guards*. How to apply *terza* to *find* on all *lines* and how to select the correct *guard* for *gaining* and maintaining control of the *advantages*, regardless of where your opponent holds their sword.

Stronger and Weaker Lines

Each *guard* has a stronger and weaker side based largely on the mechanics of the human wrist. Though it may seem that a sword pointed straight toward you could be approached on the *inside* or *outside*, it's not the case. The following exercise will help demonstrate this:

① Have your partner stand *out of measure* in *seconda*. Their *seconda* should form a straight line from their shoulder to you.

② Approach your partner and *find* their sword on your partner's *inside*. Stop at *misura larga* having found the *three advantages*.

③ Have your partner attempt to cross your sword using their *false edge*. You will attempt to resist. Your partner should cross with their *false edge* simply by pulling their point toward their *inside* while keeping their hand palm-down.

Your partner should find it easy to cross your sword, and you should find it suitably challenging to maintain a crossing of their sword without aiming well off-line from their body.

Left finds Right's seconda on the inside at misura larga.

Right easily gains the advantage of crossing on the inside with their false edge.

The *false edge* side of a *guard* is mechanically stronger for crossing. Because of this, it is generally more effective to *find* a sword against its flat, or against its *true edge*. This means its best to approach *seconda* on the *outside* and *quarta* on the *inside*. It's not impossible to *find* a sword on the opposite side; however, it requires significantly greater *crossing* and *leverage* to do so effectively.

You may wonder why we *find* swords using our *true edge* and not the false. If you acquire the *advantage of crossing* as you approach with the *true edge* the same mechanic that makes you weak on this side also allows you to engage and resist pressure more easily. It's also safer because the *true edge closes* the *line* and the *false edge* does not.

Maintaining the Debole

The position of an opponent's *debole* can sometimes make it hard to *find* or hard to maintain. The following two concepts will help you *find* and keep the advantages of *leverage* and *crossing* throughout an attack.

Finding a Palmo from the Point

When a sword is held parallel to the ground it presents two problems when you attempt to *find* it.

1. Without proper care you can lose the *advantage of leverage* by allowing your *debole* to slide into the *forte* of your opponent's sword.
2. You can easily stab yourself in the hand on your opponent's sword as you attempt to *gain*.

The answer is to make sure that you always cross your opponent's sword a hand-span (called a *palmo* in Renaissance Italian fencing manuals) from the point of their sword.

Left is holding their sword low and parallel with the ground. It is more difficult to find and the point could easily go through Right's hilt.

From the initial *finding* through to *gaining* the sword, attempt to keep your crossing at this same place. It will ensure that you maintain *leverage* and it will help you place your opponent's point beyond the rings of your *hilt* rather than inside them.

Incorrect! Right is being struck in the hand through their hilt.

Correct! Right has protected their hand by finding one palmo from the point of Left's sword.

If your opponent's blade is held quite low you may need to deepen your stance so that you can place your *hilt* more firmly beneath it, or you may need to strike downward through their sword toward a low target — more on this later.

Right has sunk lower in their posture to find a low sword.

Right aims at a lower target to gain a low sword.

Striking According to the Point

A useful tip for maintaining control of the *debole* throughout an attack is to strike a target on your opponent that is at the height of their point or higher.

For example, if your opponent has their sword in *terza* with their *hilt* at their flank and their point at the height of their shoulder, you can strike them in the shoulder, throat, or face. If their point is as high as their face, then the face would be the only target.

By striking according to the point you ensure that your *debole* will stay high and that you will increase in *leverage* as you get closer. If you choose a target that is lower than the point then during your attack the *debole* of your sword will drop down into the opponent's *forte* and you will lose the *advantage of leverage*.

Incorrect! Right has given up leverage by aiming at a target that is below the point.

Correct! Right aims at a target "according to the point" and maintains leverage.

Transports: Finding and Gaining the High Sword

If you have a particularly tall opponent, or your opponent hides their head behind their *hilt* or holds their sword particularly high, it can be difficult to *gain* and strike "according to the point". Attempting to strike under their sword without gaining it is even riskier.

Against a high sword you are safest to *find* from above but strike below. These techniques are called *transports* because they involve "transporting" your opponent's sword from one *line* into another (for example from the *high inside* to the *low outside*).

A transport from the high outside to strike the low inside.

Left defends their head using their hilt.

A transport from the high inside to strike on the low outside.

Right is struck because they did not gain Left's sword.

Exercise: Striking Against a High Seconda 🎞

As noted before, *seconda* is best approached on the *outside*.

① Start in *terza, out of measure* to your partner. They will be in *seconda*.

② Slowly approach *misura larga*, one careful step at a time. Aim to place your partner's sword on your *outside*.

③ Aim your sword at your partner's *off-side shoulder* with your point slightly above their head. This will set you up to place your partner's sword under yours (even though it is particularly high) and give you the *advantage of crossing*.

④ Cross your partner's sword and stay in their *debole*, approximately one hand-span from their point. Note: because their sword is under yours, you immediately gain the *advantage of edge*. You do not need to turn your wrist at all.

⑤ Begin applying a downward pressure with your point to their *debole*. Your goal is to force their point down and get access to the *low line*. You should now have arrived at *misura larga* and have *found* your partner's sword.

⑥ To *gain* their sword, continue to apply a downward pressure with your point, aiming at your partner's chest on their centreline, while extending into the *offensive posture* in *terza*. This should trap your partner's sword below yours with their *debole* in your *forte*.

⑦ Conduct your *thrust* with a *lunge*. Keep your *hilt* in your partner's *debole* and direct your point up into their chest.

⑧ Recover the *lunge* to *terza* or *quarta* (so you are still *gaining* your partner's sword as before).

⑩ Return to *defensive terza*, *finding* their sword as you do so.

⑪ Retreat from *measure*. Keeping your sword over your opponent's weapon throughout the entire withdrawal.

Make sure that when you get to *misura larga* you are close enough that as you move to *gain* you will catch the partner's *debole* in your *hilt*. If you are too far away your partner's point will easily slip free as you push them down.

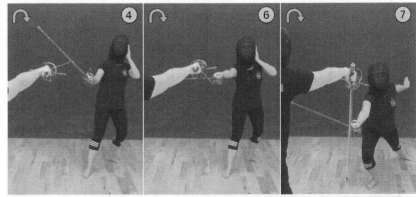

Right finds Left on the outside.   *Right presses Left down.*   *Right strikes under the sword.*

Right finds on the outside, point high ▸▸   *Right begins to push Left down* ▸▸   *Right directs their sword under the sword of Left* ▸▸   *Right gains in terza pointing down* ▸▸   *Right strikes upward into the flank of Left.*

Exercise: Striking Against a High Quarta ▦

As noted before, *quarta* is best approached on the *inside*.

① Start *out of measure* from your partner. You will be in *terza*. They will be in *quarta*.

② Slowly approach *misura larga*, one careful step at a time. Aim to place your partner's sword on your *inside*.

③ Aim your sword at your partner's *sword-shoulder* with your point slightly above their head. This will set you up to place your partner's sword under yours (even though it is particularly high) and give you the *advantage of crossing*.

④ Cross your partner's sword and stay in their *debole*, approximately one hand-span from their point. Note: because their sword is under yours, you immediately gain the *advantage of edge*. You do not need to turn your wrist at all.

⑤ Begin applying a downward pressure with your point to their *debole*. Your goal is to begin to force their point down and give you access to the *low line*. You should now have arrived at *misura larga* and have *found* your partner's sword.

⑥ To *gain* their sword, continue to apply a downward pressure with your point, aiming at your partner's chest on their *sword-side*, while extending into the *offensive posture* in *terza*. This should trap your partner's sword below yours with their *debole* in your *forte*.

⑦ If your partner's sword begins to rotate toward your *outside*, follow it by turning your hand into *seconda*, with your *hilt* high and aiming your point in the *low line* toward your partner's chest on their centreline.

⑧ Conduct your *thrust* with a *lunge*. Maintain all of the *advantages*.

⑨ Recover the *lunge* to *terza* or *seconda* (so you are still *gaining* your partner's sword as before).

⑩ Return to *defensive terza*, finding their sword as you do so.

⑪ Retreat from *measure*. Keeping your sword over your opponent's weapon throughout the entire withdrawal.

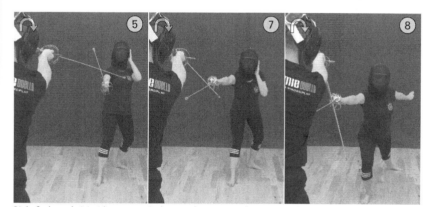

Right finds on their inside.　　*Right gains low in seconda.*　　*Right strikes with a lunge.*

Right finds on the inside, point high ▸▸　*Right pushes down Left's debole* ▸▸　*Right extends arm to seconda* ▸▸　*Right gains in seconda* ▸▸　*Right strikes with a lunge.*

Striking Against Prima

If an opponent is holding their sword in *prima* or a high *terza* you can use the same approaches as before on the *inside* or *outside*. Be aware that as you press down on their weapon you will force it to move toward your *inside* or *outside* and will need to follow this movement by going from *terza* into *quarta* or *seconda* respectively.

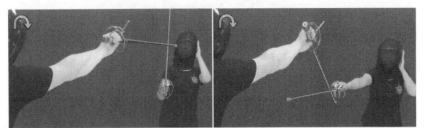

Right finds in terza on the inside, gaining on the outside in seconda.

Right finds in terza on the outside, gaining on the inside in quarta.

Right finds high terza on the inside, gaining on the outside in seconda

Keep your Hilt Low when Finding

One of the easiest traps to fall into when *finding* a high sword is to lift your *hilt* as well as your point. When you do this you expose your flank to attack and weaken your position. Always bring your opponent down to you. Elevate your point, not your *hilt*, and use the *advantage of crossing* to push your opponent down to a position of weakness.

Incorrect! Right has lifted their hilt too high. This exposes their flank.

Correct! Right keeps their hilt low and lifts their point to find.

If your opponent's sword is so high that you cannot reach it without lifting your *hilt*, threaten their flank with your point while leaning away (to keep distance). This will force your opponent to lower their sword and make it easier for you to find them.

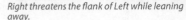

Right threatens the flank of Left while leaning away.

Left has lowered their sword to find Right. Right can more easily find them now.

Exercise: Resistance Testing

The best way to understand the application of the *three advantages* is to test them against different *guards* with resistance.

① Have your partner take a *guard*. One of the four or a variation (point higher or lower, *hilt* higher or lower).

② Approach your partner, *finding* their sword in *terza* on the *inside* or *outside*, depending on their position.

③ When you arrive at *misura larga gain* their sword.

④ Your partner will now test your position in two ways:

  • Extending their sword on its current line – Has their point been sufficiently deflected, or can they easily strike you?

  • Applying force into your position – Can they push your sword aside without a significant change of their own sword's position?

⑤ Assess any weaknesses discovered based on the *three advantages*:

  • Have you crossed their line?

  • Do you have leverage?

  • Have you applied your *true edge*?

⑥ Continue your strike to the target with a *lunge*. Have your partner test your position during and after your *lunge*.
  It's important that you keep the *advantages* throughout.

⑦ Finally recover to your *gaining* position and test it again.

⑧ Retreat *out of measure*, *finding* your partner's sword for as long as possible.

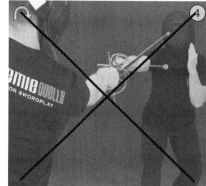 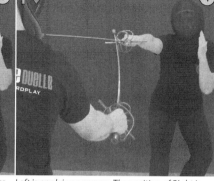

Left is applying pressure. The position of Right was incorrect and has been defeated.

Left is applying pressure. The position of Right is correct and strong.

Tips on Gaining

Be sure not to uncross the *line* as you extend to your target. As you *lunge* every one of the *advantages* should become greater, not lesser.

Incorrect! Right has uncrossed the line during their attack leaving them vulnerable. *Correct! Right has kept their point on target and maintains the advantage of crossing.*

Maintain control with your *true edge* throughout the *lunge*. If you began your *lunge* in *quarta* end it in *quarta*.

Incorrect! Right can be easily struck by their opponent during their attack. *Correct! Right keeps their true edge engaged throughout the attack and is safe.*

Keep your head tucked in behind your *hilt* and resist the urge to peak over it or around it.

Unsafe! Left has lowered their hilt exposing their head to counter-attack. *Safe! Left has positioned their hilt in front of their face. They are more fully protected from the sword of their opponent.*

Maintain the order of your *lunge*: sword, shoulders, *lunge*, recover, shoulders, sword. This will ensure that you are creating a solid defence in advance of committing your body to the attack.

Chapter Seven

Fig. 14.

I exhort unto you to practice these two things well: When being in measure against the enemy, how in time of disengaging the sword, knowing how to disengage nimbly and well, and in the time of guarding, to know how to guard equally well.

— Nicoletto Giganti, *Scola overo Teatro,* 1606

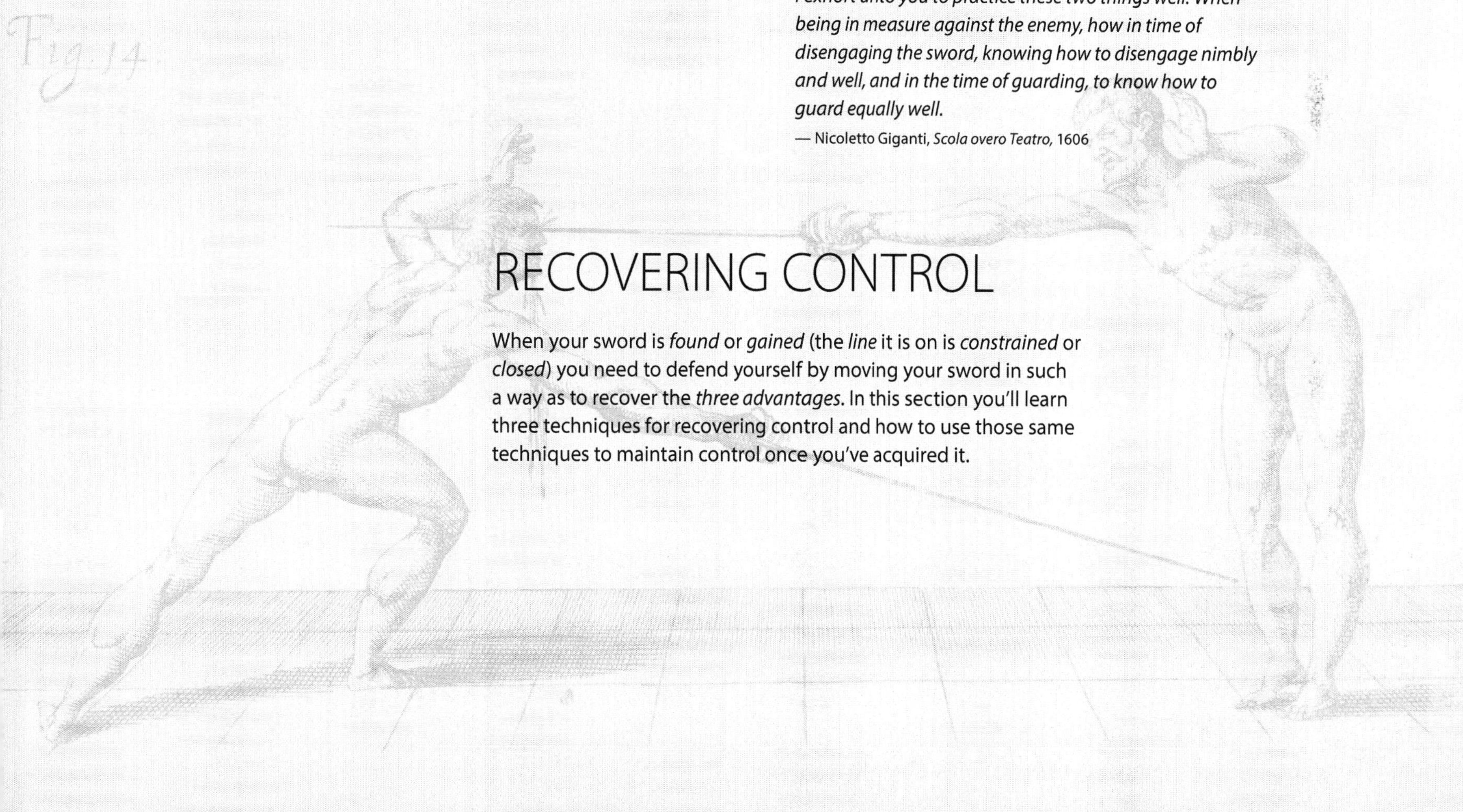

RECOVERING CONTROL

When your sword is *found* or *gained* (the *line* it is on is *constrained* or *closed*) you need to defend yourself by moving your sword in such a way as to recover the *three advantages*. In this section you'll learn three techniques for recovering control and how to use those same techniques to maintain control once you've acquired it.

Cavazione Sotto ▤

A *cavazione*[33] (in English, a "disengage") is a movement of the point of your sword from one side of your opponent's weapon to the other. You do this to leave a *constrained line* and gain an advantage of your own in an *open line*. When you have been *found*, a *cavazione* is pretty much always performed with a step backward to give you time and safety. This movement can be done over (*sopra*) or under (*sotto*) an opponent's weapon.

① You and your partner begin in *terza*, at *misura larga*, with your partner having found you on the *inside*.

② Begin a step backward and while doing so use your fingers and wrist to drop your point down and beneath your partner's blade.

③ Bring your point back up but on the *outside* of your partner's blade, and as you do so, find all *three advantages* at *misura larghissima*. Through the whole motion, both down and up, try to move only the point of your sword and not the position of your *hilt*. Stay as close to your partner's blade as possible with your point as you change *lines*.

④ If you succeeded in finding the *advantages*, advance back into *misura larga*. You have now reversed roles with your partner, and they can practice the *cavazione*.

After you've practiced this operation several times, switch to the opposite side of the sword and begin with a *finding* on the *outside*.

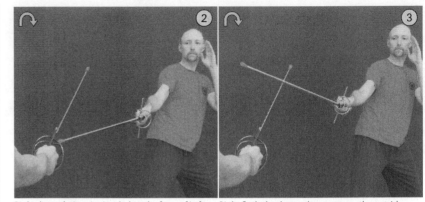

Right drops their point just below the forte of Left.   *Right finds the three advantages on the outside.*

Right has been found on the inside by Left ▸▸   *Right steps back dropping their point* ▸▸   *Right elevates their point on the outside to find Left* ▸▸   *Right steps in with control.*

Cavazione Sopra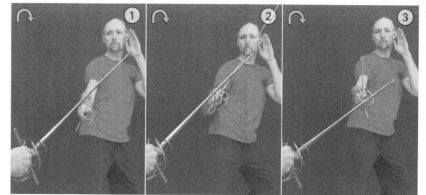

Sometimes it is faster to go over the point of your opponent's sword rather than under their blade. This motion is called a *cavazione sopra*.

① You and your partner begin in *terza*, at *misura larga*, with your partner having found you on the *outside*.

② Begin a step backward and while doing so, withdraw your forearm and use your hand and wrist to direct your point back and up, so it clears the point of your partner's sword.

③ Drop your point down on the *inside* of your partner's sword, finding the *three advantages* at *misura larghissima*. Throughout the whole motion, keep your point as close to your partner's blade as possible, and keep your forearm parallel with the ground.

④ If you have found the *three advantages*, step back into *misura larga*. You have now switched roles with your partner, and they can practice the *cavazione sopra*.

As with the *cavazione sotto*, this action can be performed on the inside as well.

Right has been found on their outside.

Right steps back and elevates their point.

Right lowers their point on the inside to find Left.

Right has been found on their outside by Left ▸▸   Right steps back and elevates their point ▸▸   Right lowers their point on the inside to find Left ▸▸   Right steps in with control.

Volta Stabile ▦

You do not necessarily need to perform a *cavazione* to regain advantage. You can recover control in the same *line* by withdrawing your sword to recover *leverage* and then pushing your opponent's sword over to recover *crossing*. This move is called a *volta stabile*,[34] in Italian, which means "stable turn" and refers to a movement where you rotate the edge of your sword from one facing to another.

① You and your partner begin in *terza*, at *misura larga*, with your partner having found you on the *inside*.

② Begin a step backward, and while doing so, withdraw your point and turn your *true edge* slightly toward your *inside*.

③ Apply pressure into your partner's *debole* as you elevate your point. The goal is to regain the *advantages of leverage* and *edge* and use those *advantages* to win the crossing. Stepping back makes it easier to *find* the opponent's *debole* and keep the point of your sword threatening.

④ Once you succeed in pushing your partner's sword aside, push only so far as you need to gain the *advantage of crossing*, then step back into *misura larga*.

Now try the *volta stabile* starting on the *outside*.

Right has been found on the inside by Left.

Right steps back and applies pressure to cross their partner's blade.

Right steps back in with control.

▦ Left approaches Right ▸▸ Right has been found on the inside by left ▸▸ Right steps back with pressure to cross Left's blade ▸▸ Right steps in with control on the inside.

While the Opponent is Finding

Performing a *cavazione* after you have been found is an important skill, however performing a *cavazione* while you are being *found* is even more effective. In this way, your opponent's plan to *find* your sword will instead result in you *finding* theirs.

① Start *out of measure* from your partner. Both of you in *terza*.

② Have your partner approach you, beginning to *find* you on your *inside*.

③ When they are about to step to *misura larga* and complete the *finding* of your sword, follow the movement of their point and perform a *cavazione* under their sword as it comes to *find* yours.

④ Bring your point up on your *outside* and *find* your partner's sword. If done correctly, your partner will complete their step to *misura larga* just as you finish *finding* their sword.

You must be prepared to act immediately after having *found* an opponent's sword. In a combative environment, there are rarely pauses at the end of a motion. An advantage you gain in one moment can be quickly lost, if you fail to act on it, in the next.

Your cavazione happens at the same time as theirs.

The same movements that allow you to recover control can also be used to help you maintain control. Here are the techniques you can use to respond to your opponent's *cavazione* or *volta stabile*. Which technique you use depends on how close you are and in which part of your blade you have been crossed.

At Larghissima – Crossed in the Debole

If your opponent pushes your sword aside using a *volta stabile*, respond with a *cavazione* and *find* their sword on the opposite *line*. Ideally, while you do this, you will also step forward and *find* their sword at a closer *measure*. (See figure below.)

If they attempt to *find* you on the opposite side of your sword with a *cavazione*, respond by making a *cavazione* of your own that finds them again in the same line. This is called a *contra-cavazione*. Ideally this is done while you step forward and gain control at a closer measure. (See figures on right.)

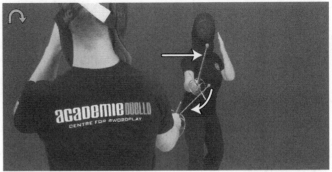

Right has made a volta stabile and Left is responding with a cavazione.

Right follows the cavazione of Left with a contra-cavazione.

Left made a volta stabile to their inside. Right countered with a cavazione to find on the outside..

Right has returned to their original position of control.

At Larga or Stretta – Crossed in the Mezza Spada

If your opponent attempts to push your sword with a *volta stabile*, when you have this crossing, hold your *finding* position firmly and step forward (see figure below on the left). If you have found correctly, they should not be able to defeat you in the same *line*. Alternately, you can respond to their pressure by *gaining* their sword (see figure below on the right). Opportunities to strike may quickly follow.

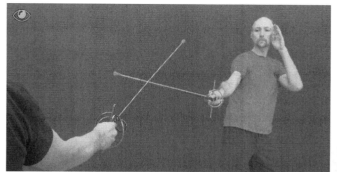

Left has found Right on their inside.

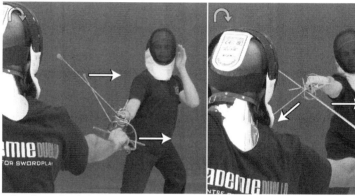

Left pushes and Right holds their position.   *Left pushes and Right gains their sword in response.*

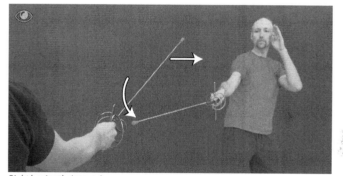

Right begins their cavazione.

If they perform a *cavazione* you can use a *volta stabile* to maintain control (see figures on right). In this case, follow your opponent's sword movement by bringing your point straight across from right to left or left to right while turning your hand. Aim to cross your opponent's sword with your *forte* over their *debole*. This will allow you to keep all *three advantages*. If your opponent is moving backward, you will need to follow them to maintain *measure* and keep *advantage*.

Anytime that you turn your edge, and redirect your point from one facing to another, it is a *volta stabile*. This is the case whether you are pushing on your opponent's sword (as you did to recover control) or following their movement, as you are here.

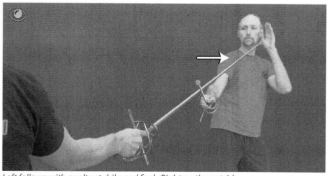

Left follows with a volta stabile and finds Right on the outside.

Football is a fencing game that allows you to practice all of the techniques of posture, movement, finding, recovering control, and maintaining control.

The setup for football is as follows:

- The "field". An area where two fencers facing one another at *misura larga* can move forward or back at least a dozen steps.
- The "end zones". Scoring areas at each side of the field.

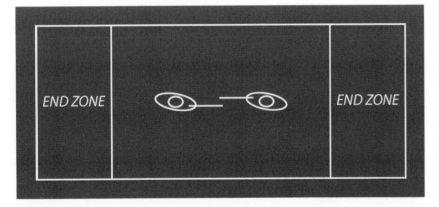

The rules:

① You and your opponent start at *misura larghissima*. You each have an end zone to your back.
② You are both seeking to *find* the sword of your opponent and drive them back into the end zone.
③ When you step into an end zone, your opponent scores a point.
④ When your opponent has *found* your sword, you must move backward.

How to play:

① Begin at *misura larghissima* with both you and your opponent in *terza*.
② The first objective is to *find* your opponent's sword at *misura larga*. You can attempt to *find* their sword and move forward, or wait and attempt to *find* them as they move forward.
③ Once someone has been *found*, the heart of the game begins. The one who has lost control must move backward and attempt to recover the *finding*; the one in control moves forward. As long as you are in a weak position, you must move backward. Should you recover control, then the roles switch and you move forward until control is lost again.
④ Once someone has been driven to the end zone, the game is over. The one who is driven to the end zone has lost.

Throughout the game both you and your opponent should maintain an awareness of *measure*. However if your opponent fails to back up when they have been *found*, you can walk your point into them to demonstrate their lack of control — make sure you are both wearing appropriate protective gear if you're using this option. Be sure to maintain an emphasis in this game on *finding*, *re-finding*, and controlling *measure*, don't focus on striking.

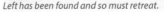
Left has been found and so must retreat.   Left has been driven into the end zone. Right wins!

Tactical: The Gaining Game

Gaining an opponent's sword allows you to defend yourself from their most direct attack and exposes them to the point of your weapon. In this game you will score by *gaining* the opponent's weapon successfully.

The setup for the gaining game:

- A 15' x 15' space that allows for both fencers to approach in and out of *measure* and circle one another.
- A fencing mask and gorget.

The rules:

1. Anytime that you form an *offensive posture* with your opponent's *debole* against your *hilt* and your point *on-line*, you score a point.
2. No attempts to strike are to be made and your weight should be maintained over your back foot throughout.
3. The winner is the first to get to 10 points. There is no requirement to reset after a point is scored.

How to play:

1. You and your opponent begin well *out of measure*.
2. The first part of the game is to attempt to *find* your opponent's sword at *misura larga*.
3. If they *find* you, use *measure* and the techniques from this section to recover control.
4. Look for a moment to *gain*. Make sure you move your sword ahead of your body and keep your hips withdrawn.
5. Continue until someone has reached 10 successful *gainings*. There is no requirement to reset after scoring. An opportunity to *gain* may come immediately after one of you has scored a point.

Left has gained the sword of Right. Left scores a point.

Right has attempted to gain but their point is not on-line. No point is scored.

Chapter Eight

The aim of fencing is the defence of self, from whence it derives its name; because 'to fence' does not mean other than defending oneself, hence it is that 'fencing' and 'defence' are words of the same meaning.

—Ridolfo Capoferro, *Gran Simulacro dell'Arte e dell'uso di Schermire*, 1610

DEFENCE AND COUNTER-OFFENCE

No matter how good you are at *finding*, recovering, and maintaining control of your opponent's weapon, you will inevitably find yourself in a position where the opponent has an opportunity to attack. Like offence, a good defence employs the *three advantages* to keep you safe and create opportunities to attack.

In this section you will learn to use *finding* and *gaining* in response to an opponent's attack in three situations:

1. When your sword is free.

2. When your sword has been *found*.

3. When your sword has been *gained*.

Defence when Free

An ideal defence is both a defence and an offence. In this way you are not only safe but you force the opponent onto the defensive, or successfully strike them and thus end the need for future defence. If your sword is free at the time of an attack, this can easily be done by *gaining* your opponent's sword.

Your sword is free when:

① You have *found* the *three advantages*, or

② Neither you nor your opponent have *found* the *three advantages*.

Left has found her opponent's sword, thus Left's sword is free and Right's is constrained.

Neither opponent has found. Thus both of their swords are free.

Defence Through Gaining

The idea of using *gaining* as a means of defending and counter-attacking will be explored in greater detail in the section on *contro-tempo* (in the following chapter).

Left has gained on the outside in response to an attack.

Exercise: Defence through Gaining

① Begin across from your partner at *misura larga*, in *terza*, on the *inside*. Neither you or your partner should *find* the sword of the other.

② Have your partner make a *lunge* toward your torso, without *finding* or *gaining* your sword.

③ In response to this attack, *gain* the sword of your partner:

  • Lead first with the point of your sword, crossing over their weapon and aiming to their right side or eye.

  • Extend your *hilt* and arm while turning your *true edge*.

  • Arrive in *quarta*, pushing your partner's sword *off-line* with your *hilt*. Be sure to keep your weight on your back leg. Do not inadvertently shift forward.

④ You should now have deflected your partner's sword and struck them simultaneously.

Practice this same exercise on the *outside*, defending by *gaining* in *seconda*.

At misura larga.   Left attacks without advantage.   Right gains the sword of left defensively.

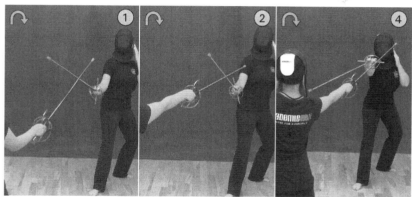

At misura larga.   Left attacks without advantage.   Right gains the sword of Left defensively.

Defence of the Leg

The best defence for your leg is distance.

① Stand across from your partner at *misura larga*, with both of you in *terza*.

② Your partner will make a *cavazione* and *thrust* at your lead leg.

③ Pull your lead leg backward away from the attack. As you pull your foot away:

- Keep your weight over your rear foot.
- Extend your sword and upper body into *seconda* (this will counterbalance your leg).
- Rest your evading leg about three foot-lengths behind your rear foot, on the ball of the foot.

④ If there is opportunity, deliver a simultaneous *thrust* to your opponent's sword arm, chest, or face.

⑤ Recover by either passing backward, or replacing your leg in front of you.

In this defence, be sure to keep your weight over your back leg (your left if you are holding your sword in your right hand). You will simply swing the lead leg away from the attack while your upper body rocks forward. Keeping your weight on the left leg makes the action faster and allows you to extend your sword forward without losing *measure*.

Incorrect! If you put your weight onto the evading leg you will lose measure.

Correct! The leg is voided and the opponent is struck simultaneously.

Defence from Control

It is always safer to have *found* your opponent's sword whenever you are in *measure*. In this way you can more easily defend yourself even if your opponent seeks to *gain* your sword as they attack.

In this exercise you are going to practice *gaining* in response to your partner's attack, as you did before, but starting instead from a position where you have the *three advantages*.

Exercise: Maintaining and Gaining

① Begin by *finding* your partner's sword on your *inside* or *outside* at *misura larga*.

② Your partner's job, in the first part of the exercise, is to *advance* and *retreat* while disengaging between the *inside* and *outside lines*. Your job is to maintain control of their sword, using the techniques from the Recovering Control section, while moving to stay at *misura larga*.

③ Periodically your partner will attempt to *gain* your sword and strike in their current *line*, even though you have already *found* them and the *line* is *constrained*. Your partner must always move their sword directly forward. Their role is to test your position, not attempt to recover control.

④ As soon as you sense that your partner has begun their attack (through visual or tactile information), *gain* their sword. In this way, you should simultaneously defend yourself and strike them.

When you *gain*, be sure to keep your point on target and your blade crossing your partner's. The easiest way to lose the crossing of your partner's sword is to push with your *hilt* while allowing your point to be slack. By maintaining firm control over the point of your sword you'll prevent your partner from winning the crossing.

Right has found Left on their outside. *Left has attempted to strike and Right has gained in response.*

Right has found Left on their outside. *Left has attempted to strike and Right has gained in response.*

You may wonder why someone would attack into your sword when you have the *three advantages*. This could occur simply because your opponent is not aware that you have control or because they believe they can defeat you in spite of your advantage. And, if you don't practice exercises like this one, they will.

Defence when Found

You have practiced using *finding* to make the way safe for attack, and to prevent your opponent from easily attacking you. Now you will learn to use *finding* to defend yourself from an attack where your opponent has the *three advantages*. This type of *finding* is often called a "parry"[35] or in Italian a *parata*.

Exercise: Finding in Response to an Attack on the Inside

① Begin at *misura larga*, with your partner having *found* your sword on your *inside* in *terza*.

② Your partner will begin an attack by *gaining* your sword in *quarta* and beginning a *lunge*.

③ As they begin their *lunge*, you will *find* their sword by performing a *volta stabile*:

• Turn your *true edge* toward their blade (to find the *advantage of true edge*)

• withdraw your forearm back slightly by bending at the elbow and elevate your point at your wrist to cross their *debole* (to find the *advantage of leverage*),

• then cross over their weapon by pushing their sword to your *inside* and down with your *mezza spada* over their *debole* (to find the *advantage of crossing*).

④ Retreat during this action to give yourself more time and space.

⑤ You will now have *found* your opponent's sword on your *inside* and successfully negated their attack.

Left has found on their inside. Left gains on their inside and begins their attack. Right parries by withdrawing and finding on the inside.

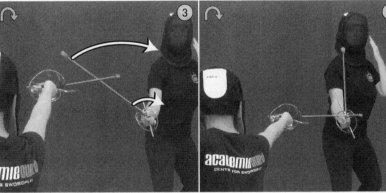

Right parries by moving their point up and across to the inside. Right has successfully parried the attack.

Exercise: Finding in Response to an Attack on the Outside

① Begin at *misura larga*, with your partner having *found* your sword on your *outside* in *terza*.

② Your partner will begin an attack by *gaining* your sword in *seconda* and beginning a *lunge*.

③ As they begin their *lunge*, you will *find* their sword by performing a *volta stabile*:

- Turn your *true edge* toward their blade (to find the *advantage of true edge*)

- withdraw your forearm back slightly by bending at the elbow and elevate your point at your wrist to cross their *debole* (to find the *advantage of leverage*),

- then cross over their weapon by pushing their sword to your *outside* and down, using your *mezza spada* over their *debole* (to find the *advantage of crossing*).

④ Retreat during this action to give yourself more time and space.

⑤ You will now have *found* your opponent's sword on your *outside* and successfully negated their attack.

Left has found on their outside.

Left gains on their outside and begins their attack.

Right parries by withdrawing and finding on the outside.

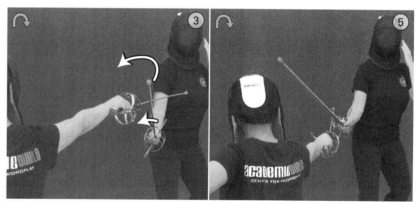

Right parries by moving their point up and across to the outside.

Right has successfully parried the attack.

Finding and Stepping Forward

Stepping backward gives you more time to defend, however it also adds more time to your potential counter-attack. This could make it easier for your opponent to defend themselves or simply to escape. If you are of equal or greater reach than your opponent, this may not be a problem. However if you are at a reach disadvantage you may need to use your opponent's attack as a moment to gain a closer *measure*.

To *find* and step forward you must use the same technique as above, however, as your partner attacks you must do one of two things to stay safe:

① *Find/parry* their sword at the beginning of their attack without moving, then step forward before their attack has concluded.

Right parries without stepping back.

Right gains the sword of Left and begins their counter-attack from misura stretta.

② *Find* their sword while they attack (potentially with a small retreating step) and then move in quickly while they recover. At the end of their recovery you should be at a closer *measure* and in a position of control.

Right parries with a small withdrawing step.

Right follows the recovery of Left with a passing step, to get to a closer measure.

It is *essential* in these techniques that you begin your defence with the point of your sword and not your *hilt* or your body. You must also have your opponent's point pushed aside before you begin to enter. If you attempt to step in, or push with your *hilt*, before finding the *advantage of crossing*, you will step onto your opponent's point.

Defence when Gained

Sometimes it's too late to use a *volta stabile* to parry, in these instances you need to use a different type of defence called a "yield". In a yield you allow your opponent to push your *debole* aside and then lift your hilt to protect your head and body by using your sword like a sloped roof.

Right has yielded by dropping their point and lifting their hilt.

The most common circumstances for this to occur are:

1. When your opponent has *gained* your sword and has already begun their attacking movement forward before you begin to *parry*. (See figure below on the left).
2. When your opponent has *found* your sword at a close *measure*, like *misura stretta*, and begins their attack before you are able to back up.
3. When you have begun attacking your opponent and lose the *three advantages* in the middle of your attack. (See figure below on the right).

After you yield, you will continue the circular motion of your blade to place it over your opponent's weapon or, in some cases, strike. The yield and circular cutting motion of your blade are together called a *stramazzone*.[36]

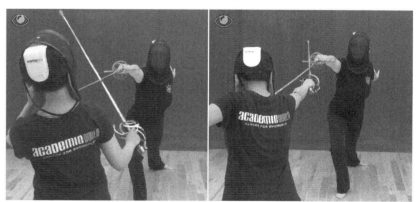

Left is too close at this stage of the attack to use a volta stabile to parry.

Left has lost the three advantages while attacking. They do not have enough time to parry with a volta stabile.

Performing a Stramazzone Starting on the Outside ▦

① Begin by having your partner *find* your sword on your *outside*, at *misura larga*.

② Begin an attack by extending your sword. Have your partner respond to your extension by *gaining* your sword in *seconda* and *lunging*.

③ Turn your hand into *prima*. Let your point drop under your partner's pressure while continuing to lift your *hilt* in front of your face. Your point will be aimed down at the ground. This will push your partner's point from the *outside* of your arm to the *inside*.

④ Deflect your partner's point past your head on your *inside* using your *forte*.

⑤ Keep your arm extended. Pull your point around in a wheel-like motion, past your off-side shoulder, then forward and down so that you cross your partner's sword, in their *debole*, with your *true edge* on your *inside*. Side-step toward your *outside* while you do this.

⑥ Find the *three advantages* over your partner's sword and lower your sword into *terza*.

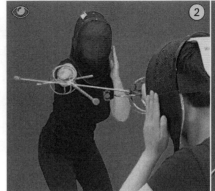
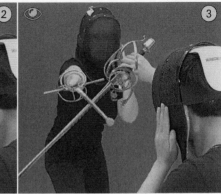

Right has been gained on their outside and is about to be struck.

Right lifts their hilt and drops their point to push Left's sword past on their inside.

Right has been gained by Left ▸▸ *Right drops their point and lifts their hilt* ▸▸ *Right continues to circle their sword* ▸▸ *Left's sword has passed without hitting* ▸▸ *Right finishes the circle and finds Left's sword while stepping back.*

Performing a Stramazzone Starting on the Inside

① Begin by having your partner *find* your sword on your *inside*, at *misura larga*.

② Begin an attack by extending your sword. Have your partner respond to your extension by *gaining* your sword in *quarta* and *lunging*.

③ Turn your hand into *quarta*. Let your point drop under your partner's pressure while continuing to lift your *hilt* in front of your face. This will require that you slightly open and relax your hand. Your point will be aimed down at the ground and toward your *outside*. This will push your partner's point from the *inside* of your arm to the *outside*.

④ Deflect your partner's point past your head on your *outside* using your *hilt* and *forte*.

⑤ Keep your arm extended. Pull your point around in a wheel-like motion, past your sword-side shoulder, then forward and down so that you cross your partner's sword, in their *debole*, with your *true edge* on your *outside*. Side-step toward your *inside* while you do this.

⑥ Find the *three advantages* over your partner's sword and lower your sword into *terza*.

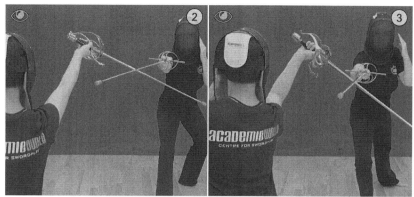

Left begins to yield by dropping their point and moving Right's sword from their inside to their outside.

Left lifts their hilt and drops their point to push Right's sword past on their inside.

As you practice these techniques, you may see that you could perform the *stramazzone* and cut down onto your partner's head or arms, instead of covering their sword. Though this is true, it is best at this point in your training to seek to control your partner's weapon. If you seek to strike with a cut, your partner could still hit you with a *thrust* because you have not controlled their sword. Defence first.

Right has been gained by Left on the inside ▶▶ Right drops their point and lifts their hilt ▶▶ Right continues to circle their sword ▶▶ Left's sword has passed without hitting ▶▶ Right finishes the circle and finds Left's sword while stepping back.

Chapter Nine

The reason why the name tempo was given to the movements made while fencing is that the time employed to make one movement cannot be employed to make any other. Therefore, if your opponent makes a movement within the distances while you see an opening and are ready to strike, you will surely wound him, because it is not possible for him to make two movements at one time.

—Salvator Fabris, *Lo Schermo*, 1606

TEMPO

Time is the essential building block in the music of fencing. Just like in a musical piece, the nature of an engagement changes dramatically based on its pacing, when you play the notes, and how long each is sustained.

A real fight does not have a set rhythm. You must both match and move in discord from the other player. You must draw your opponent into your music and then change it suddenly.

In this section we'll explore the theory of tempo and how to practically apply that theory to lead your opponent into error and strike them.

Three Meanings for Tempo

Tempo, which is the Italian word for time, is a blanket term in Italian fencing that refers to all of the connections between time and motion. There are three primary meanings that we will explore in relation to fencing:

1. Rhythm.

The *tempo* of a fight can be thought of as a series of turns in a game, or as a dance where the movements of each combatant move in-step with the beating of a drum. The speed or syncopation of the drum sets the *tempo* of the fight, and to be moving within its rhythm is to be moving "in tempo". Knowing when to be in rhythm and when to break rhythm is an essential part of fighting.

2. Opportunity.

Having good timing for an action is nearly as important as having good form for that action. An attack has the best opportunity of being successful if it is done in a moment where the opponent cannot defend. The right moment is also critical to preventing your opponent from striking you.

3. Proportion.

The speed of a particular motion is not as important as its length. All things being equal, a shorter motion will conclude faster than a longer motion. The comparison of the proportional size of one motion to another is essential to both managing your own safety and forcing your opponent into error. You always want to make movements that are equal to or smaller than those of your opponent. One of the most common ways to control proportion is by controlling the distance that your opponent must move their point in order to strike. This is done through controlling *measure* and through *finding* the opponent's sword. This connection of controlling *measure* to control *tempo* is an essential part of both successful defence and offence.

Tempo as Rhythm

Any combative action can be divided up into a series of individual movements or *tempos* ("tempi" in Italian). A movement has a beginning, an end, and a straight path of travel in between. An example of a one *tempo* movement would be extending your arm from *terza* into *quarta*, or moving your front foot forward a foot-length.

As soon as you stop moving or change direction one *tempo* ends and another begins. To extend your sword in *quarta*, then having arrived there, move into *seconda*, would take two *tempos*, no matter how quickly you conducted the change.

Movements can share a single *tempo* if they happen simultaneously. Extending your arm and taking a step forward at the same time would be a one *tempo* action. However, if you extend your arm while stationary, and then step, you will have used two *tempos*.

Extending from defensive terza directly into offensive quarta takes one tempo.

Extending into offensive terza and then turning the hand into quarta takes two tempos.

Exercise: Exchanging Full Tempi

In this exercise you and your partner will have a sword fight. You will conduct this sword fight like you are playing a turn-based game. Only one of you will be able to conduct a fencing move at a time, and the other will remain in place until this move is concluded. Each movement or "turn" will be one *tempo* in length.

For the purposes of our game, a single *tempo* will be the length of time it takes to make one *advancing step* (forward foot followed by back foot). On your turn, you can perform an *advancing step*, or any action that is equal in time to an *advancing step*. For example, transitioning from one *guard* to another, half of a *passing step*, or a *lunge*. If the action can be conducted simultaneously with the *advancing step*, you may perform them together; for example, taking an *advancing step* forward while changing *guards*.

To play this game:

① Start in a *guard* and *out of measure* from your opponent.

② Take *one-tempo* turns, alternating back and forth.

③ Continue alternating until you or your opponent has been struck.

④ Reset the game by moving *out of measure*.

You can only move on your turn. If your opponent is about to conduct a wounding action to you, and it is not your turn, you must simply stand and take it. Observe the situation and determine how you could avoid the same demise in the next round.

Examples of Single Tempo Actions

An advancing step.

Half a passing step.

A lunge from Terza.

Exercise: Exchanging Half Tempi

Conduct the same exercise again, but shorten the length of each *tempo*. Now a single *tempo* will be equal to the movement of only one foot's step. This means:

① An *advancing step* will take two turns to conduct, one for the front foot, one for the back.

② A *lunge* must be conducted in two parts, the upper body and then the step, or the step and then the shift forward.

③ Moving from one *line* to another takes a turn. So if you are on the *inside* and you desire to strike on the *outside* you will need to perform a *cavazione* in one turn and strike in the next.

Movements Done in Half Tempos

An advancing step takes two turns:

1. The front foot moves,   2. The back foot moves.

An attack at misura larga takes two turns:

1. Extend to offense,   2. Lunge.

Exercise: Sharing Full Tempi

Though the alternating tempo game is useful for understanding an aspect of *tempo*, combat is more of a dance than a turn-based game. To dance a waltz with a partner you must move with the rhythm of the music and in-time with your partner. As they take a step forward, you take a step back, as they step away, you step forward, responding to each of their movements in the same moment. When you match rhythm with your opponent and move when they move, you are moving "in-tempo".

In this exercise, you will move in full *tempos* as we did in the first exchanging tempos exercise, except this time you and your opponent will be acting simultaneously. As in the previous exercise, your objective is to outsmart your opponent and use good sword fighting technique and strategy to defeat them.

Before beginning this next game, designate a leader for the game. It is beneficial if the leader can be a non-participating third party.

① Stand in a *guard* and *out of measure* from your opponent.

② You and your opponent plan a single *tempo* action in your minds.

③ The leader, after giving both participants a moment or two to come up with their plans, says "go."

④ At the same time, you and your opponent conduct the single *tempo* action you had planned. If you had not come up with anything you stay still. Do not change your action based on your opponent's action. To learn from the drill you must conduct it exactly as planned. Be sure to conduct the action with care and safety.

⑤ Think of your next action and act when instructed. Continue this process until you or your opponent has succeeded in striking the other.

To truly gain all you can from this exercise, it is vital that you act honestly within its rules. Don't change your intent mid-motion, instead try to think ahead and out-strategize your opponent.

After you have played the game a few times, have the leader shorten the amount of time allowed for planning in between each turn. As you shorten the planning time, the apparent "speed" of the game will increase. The shorter the time for planning, the quicker the rhythm, and the more like combat the game will become.

Left has been caught "in-tempo" by Right.

Tempo as Opportunity

Here is a simple problem: Your opponent is standing at *misura larga*. They are close enough to be struck with a *lunge*. You push forward into your *lunge*, yet as you commit to the attack, your opponent simply steps back out of your *measure* and you fall short.

An alternate problem: You *lunge*, but as you do so, your opponent *finds* your sword, negating its ability to strike, and leaving you in a position of disadvantage.

Both of these defences are relatively easy to conduct and require very little energy on the part of your opponent. So how do you overcome these challenges and succeed in an attack?

To find an opportunity to successfully strike, you need to understand the moments where it is most difficult for your opponent to effectively defend themselves or strike you in response. All of these *tempos of opportunity* have two ingredients:

1. Your opponent is in a *measure* where you can strike them.
2. Your opponent is moving in a committed and predictable manner.

These two ingredients come together in four specific ways which are called the *four tempos* which you will explore throughout this section.

Note: The *tempos* you are about to learn are described in slightly different ways in different historical sources and modern schools. See the glossary section for more information on their use.

Primo Tempo

The word *primo* in Italian means "first". The first *tempo* when an opponent can be struck is as they step into your *measure* — in particular your *misura larga*. If you attack as an opponent steps forward it negates their ability to step away. It also makes it much more difficult for them to defend themselves with their sword.

Exercise: Striking in Primo Tempo

Your partner in this exercise will use their hand as a target for you to strike. It does not require that they have a sword.

① Have your partner begin out of *measure*. They will present their hand as a target.

② You will stand in *terza* and wait as your partner approaches one confident *advancing step* at a time.

③ As your partner begins to lift their foot to step into your *misura larga*, begin your attack. In this way, your attack should strike, as your partner's foot lands in *misura larga*.

④ As soon as your partner sees you begin to *lunge*, they will attempt to step away. If you have not timed your attack correctly, they will succeed in stepping back out of *misura larga*. If you have timed your attack correctly, they will be unable to step away because their body will already be moving forward.

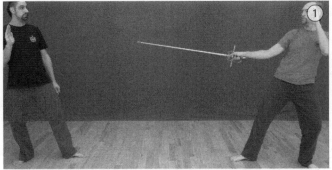

Start out of measure.

Right begins attacking as soon as Left lifts his foot.

Right strikes Left's hand as it arrives in measure.

Exercise: Striking in Primo Tempo Through the Sword

In this version of the *primo tempo* exercise, your partner will have a sword and will advance while threatening you with their point.

① Have your partner begin *out of measure* in *terza*.

② You will stand in *terza* and wait as your partner approaches one confident *advancing step* at a time.

③ *Find* your partner's sword while they approach. Before they arrive at your *misura larga* you should have already begun to acquire all *three advantages*.

④ As your partner begins their step into your *misura larga*, gain their sword in *quarta* or *seconda* (depending on which line you are in), then strike them in *primo tempo*.

⑤ As soon as your partner sees you begin to *lunge*, they will attempt to step away. They will also attempt to direct their point at your chest. In this way, they will both test your ability to strike in *primo tempo* and to properly *gain* their sword as you do so.

Right begins to find at misura larghissima.   *Left begins their step.*   *Right strikes Left in primo tempo.*

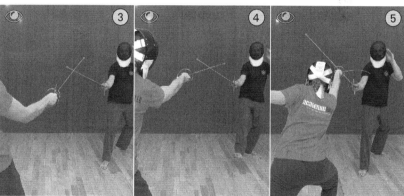

Left begins to find at misura larghissima.   *Right begins their step.*   *Left strikes right in primo tempo.*

Exercise: Cavazione in Tempo (Disengage in Time) 🎞️

You don't have to *find* your opponent's sword as they approach to successfully strike them in *primo tempo*. In this version of the exercise, you will allow your partner to try to *find* your sword. As they begin *finding* you will strike them in *primo tempo* using a *cavazione* to *gain* their sword in the opposite *line*.

① Have your partner begin *out of measure* in *terza*.

② You will stand in *terza* and wait as your partner approaches one confident *advancing step* at a time.

③ As your partner approaches, allow them to *find* your sword on the *inside* or *outside*.

④ As your partner begins their step into your *misura larga*, perform a *cavazione* under their sword to the opposite *line* and immediately move forward to *gain* their sword and strike (gaining all three of the *advantages* as you do so). In this way, you will *gain* their weapon and strike them in *primo tempo*. Extend your point forward at the same time as you conduct your *cavazione*. This will make your *cavazione* into a corkscrew, or spiral, shape, allowing you to both make the *cavazione* and *gain* in the same *tempo*. If you *cavazione*, and then *gain*, as two distinct movements, your action will take two *tempos* to complete. This will give your opponent a free *tempo* to step away or *find* your sword.

⑤ As soon as your partner sees you begin to *lunge*, they will attempt to step away. They will also attempt to direct their point at your chest. In this way, they will test both your ability to strike in *primo tempo*, and to properly *gain* their sword as you do so.

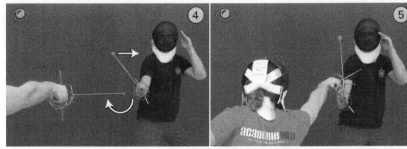

Left begins to disengage as Right seeks to find.   *Left gains and strikes before the end of Right's step.*

Efficient and precise movement is the key to being successful. I recommend spending time conducting simply the mechanical part of this exercise (conducting the *cavazione* and *gaining* in one *tempo*) with your partner fixed in place, then bring in the aspect of *tempo*.

These exercises should be conducted slowly before you accelerate them in speed. It is also essential that the approaching partner move in a committed and consistent manner and not speed up to avoid being struck.

🎞️   *At larghissima* ▸▸ *Left steps to find*   *Right begins their cavazione* ▸▸ *Left continues forward*   *Right gains left and* ▸▸ *begins their attack*   *Right strikes Left in primo tempo.*

Tempo as Proportion

A Proportion Problem: You are standing in *terza*. Your opponent takes a small and discrete step into your *misura larga*. During this step you attempt to strike them in *primo tempo*. Your opponent, however, completes their step and steps away before your attack has time to hit them.

Left steps into misura larga with an advance.   *Right gains and begins their attack.*   *Left steps away and avoids being struck.*

As stated in the introduction to this section, you want to make sure that your movements are equal to or lesser in length to those of your opponent. A *lunge* from *terza* is quite a long movement, especially when compared to an *advancing step*, if that step is small and judicious. In the above example the fencer on the left may have stepped forward in error, but they are able to realize their error and exit before being struck because the attacker's movement is proportionally longer.

To successfully strike in *primo tempo* the attacker must shorten the length of their attack so it is proportionally equal to that of the step.

Exercise: Primo Tempo and Proportion 🎞

First, experiment with the proportion problem that was just outlined by practicing the *primo tempo* exercise with your partner taking smaller steps. You will attempt to strike from *terza* as they step to *misura larga*. They will step away, even when your timing is right (as long as you both move at the same speed, you should experience the proportion problem).

Now you will solve the proportion problem by *gaining* your opponent's sword before they step to *misura larga*. In this way you will have shortened the length of your attack.

① Have your partner begin *out of measure* in *terza*.

② You will stand in *terza* and wait as your partner approaches one step at a time.

③ *Find* your partner's sword while they approach.

④ As your opponent steps to *misura larghissima*, gain their sword in *seconda* or *quarta* (choose the *guard* that is appropriate to the *line* they are in).

⑤ As your partner begins their step into your *misura larga*, lunge.

By *gaining* your partner's sword before they step to *misura larga* you are shortening the length of movement you must make to strike them. During their step to *misura larga* all you need to do is step. This significantly reduces your partner's time to respond.

🎞 Start out of measure ▸▸ Left approaches   ▸▸ Left steps to larghissima   Right gains ▸▸ Left steps to larga   Right begins lunge ▸▸   Right strikes in a short primo tempo.

Due-tempi 🎞

Due-tempi ("two-tempos" in English) is the opportunity to strike your opponent in two motions. In the first *tempo* you displace your opponent's sword from the *line*, and in the second, you strike them as they bring their sword back *on-line*.

Exercise: Beat and Attack

In this exercise, you will strike your opponent's sword with a *beat* that will give you an opportunity to then strike the opponent as they bring their sword back *on-line*.

① Begin with your partner at *misura larga*, with both your swords parallel on the *inside*, in *terza*. Leave six to twelve inches of space between your blades.

② Turn your *true edge* toward your partner's sword (with your hand slightly palm-up), then strike their *debole* with your own by forcefully flicking your wrist. If done successfully, your partner's point will be sent away from you.

③ You will immediately move into *quarta*, placing your hilt between your partner's sword and your body. You are essentially *gaining* the space that your partner's sword must return to.

④ Having *gained*, you will proceed into your *lunge*, striking your partner in the chest or face.

⑤ After their sword is beaten, your partner will attempt to bring their point back to the *line*, directing it at your face or chest. Your job done correctly, they will encounter your *hilt* or *forte*, and be struck in that moment.

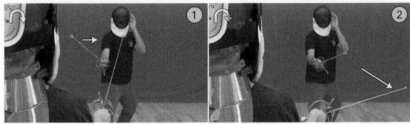

Right begins their beat.   *Right beats. Left's sword is displaced by the beat.*

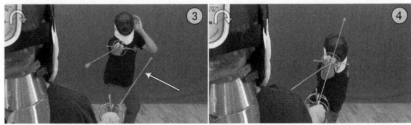

Left attempts to return their sword. Right extends.   *Right strikes while gaining the returning sword.*

Avoid moving your *debole* away from your partner's sword before conducting your beat (winding up). If you make this error, you may give your partner a tempo to strike you, instead of one for you to strike them.

Right begins their beat ▸▸ *Left's sword is displaced by the beat*   ▸▸ *Left attempts to return their sword*   *Right extends* ▸▸   *Right strikes while gaining the returning sword.*

Exercise: Parata-Risposta ▤

A *parry*, or *parata*, as we explored before, is the act of *finding* your opponent's sword in response to their attack. A *risposta* is an attack of your own conducted immediately following a *parry*, while your opponent attempts to bring their sword back *on-line*.

① Begin at *misura larga* with your partner having *found* your sword on the *inside* in *terza*.

② Your partner will begin an attack by *gaining* your sword in *quarta* and beginning a *lunge*.

③ As they begin their *lunge*, you will *find* their sword by performing a *volta stabile*:

- Turn your *true edge* toward their blade (to find the *advantage of true edge*)
- withdraw and elevate your point by pulling your arm back slightly at the elbow (to acquire the *advantage of leverage*),
- and cross over their weapon by pushing their sword to your *inside* and down, using your *mezza spada* over their *debole* (to acquire the *advantage of crossing*).
- Retreat during this action to give you more time and space.

④ Having *found* the opponent's sword, you will immediately extend into *quarta*, *gaining* it.

⑤ As the opponent attempts to bring their sword back *on-line* and recover from their *lunge*, you will proceed with a *lunge*, striking them in the chest or face in *due-tempi*.

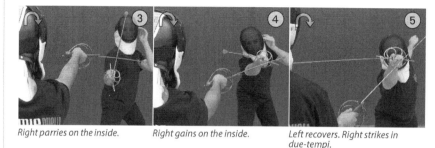

Right parries on the inside. Right gains on the inside. Left recovers. Right strikes in due-tempi.

It is essential that you *find* the sword exactly as you would if you were approaching. Don't over-lift your point, or send your sword strongly *off-line*.

Conducting a Parata-Risposta on the Outside

Right parries on the outside. Right gains on the outside. Left recovers. Right strikes in due-tempi.

▤ Left gains the sword of Right ▸▸ Left attacks Right begins to parry ▸▸ Right fully finds the sword of Left ▸▸ Left recovers Right gains ▸▸ Right strikes in due-tempi.

Over-gathering the arm

Incorrect! Right's elbow is too close to their flank.   *Correct! Right has stepped back to parry.*

Be sure to leave at least a hand-span of distance between your elbow and your side. If you need to withdraw your weapon further in order to gain the *advantage of leverage*, step back while parrying instead.

Defensive only

Incorrect! Right has pointed their sword upward.   *Correct! Right has parried by finding with point on-line.*

It is essential that you threaten your opponent at all times. Keep your point in a threatening place even when defending.

Forgetting to gain before reposting

Incorrect! Right has attacked without gaining.   *Correct! Right has gained before attacking.*

Always *gain* in proper order, with your sword and then shoulders extending before you step. In this way, if you fail you have warning and can abort.

Parrying with the Hilt Instead of the Point

Incorrect! Right has parried with their hilt to the inside.   *Correct! Right has parried by using their point and has kept their hilt in front of their body.*

The *advantage of crossing* is the most powerful of the *three advantages* in the *thrust*. Be sure to use your point to cross the opponent's sword and push them down with your blade. Do not push your *hilt* to the *inside* or *outside* to *parry*. This will make it easier for your opponent to cross you.

Tactical: Primo Tempo vs Due-tempi

In this game one side is going to attempt to strike in *primo tempo*, the other, in *due-tempi*.

① Begin *out of measure* from your opponent, in *terza*.

② Both of you may move forward and back. Your first objective is to perceive the moment that your opponent steps into your *misura larga*, and strike them in *primo tempo*.

③ Your opponent's objective is to fool your sense of *measure*, or your timing, so that you miss the *primo tempo* opportunity and attack too late. When you attack, they will attempt to *find* your sword, and conduct a *parata-risposta*.

④ If you fail in striking in *primo tempo*, seek to recover quickly and move back *out of measure*. In this way, your opponent will need to step forward again and give you the *primo tempo* opportunity a second time.

⑤ Once someone has succeeded in striking, switch roles.

Right is stepping into misura larga. Left is beginning an attack in primo tempo.

Left has attacked out of tempo. Right has successfully parried.

Contro-tempo

One of the moments when your opponent is most vulnerable is as they move to strike you. The opportunity that occurs during an opponent's attack is called *contro-tempo*. Successful *contro-tempo* has two components:

1. The *tempo* of your attack is of equal or lesser *proportion* to your opponent's.
2. Your attack defends you from the opponent's attack. This is generally done by acquiring the *three advantages*.

Exercise: Striking in Simple Contro-tempo

As we explored in the section on defence and counter-offence, if an opponent does not seek to control the *three advantages*, they may be vulnerable to being struck in *contro-tempo*.

① Begin across from your partner at *misura larga*, in *terza*, on the *inside*, with no *advantages* acquired by either of you.

② Have your partner make a straight *thrust* toward your torso, without *finding* or *gaining* your sword.

③ Simultaneously with this attack, *gain* the sword of your partner in *quarta* by aiming a strike at their right shoulder or eye. Lead first with the point of your sword, then extend the *hilt* and arm, while turning your *true edge*, and pushing your *hilt* to your *inside* to *close the line*. If done properly, this will deflect your partner's sword and you will hit them in *contro-tempo*.

There are no new techniques here—you are *finding* and *gaining* your partner's sword as you have done previously, but now with an added element of timing. Start slowly, always maintaining order and precision.

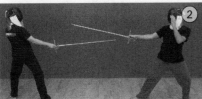

Left begins their attack without cover.   *Right gains and strikes in contro-tempo.*

Contro-tempo Drill

Now you will attempt to strike in *contro-tempo* against attacks to random targets.

① Stand with your partner at their *misura larga* with your swords parallel. No *advantages* have been found by either party.

② Your partner will attack you with a *lunge* to a target of their choosing, *inside* or *outside*, high or low. They will do this without attempting to *gain* your sword.

③ If your partner attacks your *high inside*, you will *gain* and strike in *quarta*. If your partner attacks your *high outside*, you will *gain* and strike in *seconda*. If your partner attacks in your *low line*, you will withdraw the leg and strike in *seconda*. Note that withdrawing the leg protects the hip and belly as well. See the three images below.

④ Have your partner recover and attack in a new *line*. You will return to *terza* along with them and be immediately prepared to *gain* their new attack.

Right strikes in quarta against an attack on the inside.   *Right strikes in seconda against an attack on the outside.*   *Right strikes with a leg void.*

Stringere: Strategic Constraint

Even with a limit of three *lines* (*high inside*, *high outside*, *low*) perceiving and successfully responding to an attack in *contro-tempo* can be challenging. You need a way to force your opponent into a predictable attack, that is proportionally larger than your counter-attack, so your chance to succeed in *contro-tempo* is more assured.

When you *find* your opponent's sword you put yourself in a position of mechanical strength over their current position. This eliminates one of your opponent's potential *lines of attack* and puts them in a position where they must move to an *open line* in order to strike. This move takes time and makes their next action much more predictable. This operation of strategic constraining is called *stringere*[37] in Italian, pronounced STREEN-jair-eh, with the emphasis on the first syllable.

Stringere has three components:

1. Constraint. Placing your opponent's weapon in a position of weakness in its current *line*. Now the opponent cannot easily strike the targets directly *in-line* with their sword, and your *lines* for striking them are *open*.

2. Invitation. When you *constrain* one *line*, for example your *inside line*, you must leave the other *line* open, in this case your *outside line*. This *open line* is the best place for your opponent to attempt to gain control or strike. Knowing this allows you to more easily predict and respond to the opponent's next action.

3. Proportion. Having *constrained* one set of options and made another set of options more appetizing, you must control the amount of time that it takes for your opponent to move from one option to the other. The goal is to make their movement between *lines* larger than your response to counter it.

Left has constrained Right on their outside. Right must move their point a proportionally larger distance to escape from constraint.

Right has constrained Left on their outside. Left must move their point a proportionally larger distance to find an open line.

Exercise: Contro-tempo and Stringere 🎞

In this exercise, you will use *stringere* to make the next action of your partner more predictable and easier to respond to.

① Start *out of measure* from your partner with both of you in *terza*.

② Approach your partner and *find* them on your *inside* at *misura larga*.

③ Your partner will now attempt to make a *cavazione*, *gain*, and strike on your *outside line* in *seconda*.

Right has found Left on their inside. *Right follows the disengage of Left.*

④ While your partner performs their *cavazione*, follow it with a *volta stabile* while you extend your arm and upper body:

- Start first by moving your point from the *inside* to the *outside*. Stay over top of your partner's sword.
- Aim toward a target that gives you *crossing* and extend your arm as you do so to increase your *leverage*.

- Catch your partner's *debole* on your *mezza spada* below your sword.
- Lift their *debole* up and push it to your *outside* with your *forte* and *hilt* as you turn your hand into *seconda*. You're able to succeed at *gaining* your partner's sword while they make a *cavazione* because their action is proportionally longer than yours.

⑤ At this point, your partner may have already run onto the point of your sword; if they have not, help the process along by making a *firm-footed lunge*. All of this should have happened in the time of your partner's attack and thus be in *contro-tempo*.

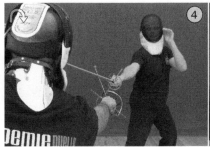

Right begins to gain on the outside. *Right gains and strikes in contro tempo in seconda.*

⑥ Recover back into *seconda* and then into *terza*, maintaining the *three advantages* as long as possible while you retreat *out of measure*.

| 🎞 | Right has found Left on their inside ▸▸ | Left disengages to strike ▸▸ | Right follows the disengage with their point ▸▸ | Right gains in seconda and strikes in contro tempo ▸▸ | Right recovers and finds Left's sword. |

Practice the same exercise on the *inside* and *outside*. The most essential element is beginning the *volta stabile* with a movement of your point so that you are always winning the *advantage of crossing* first. Secondly, be sure that you are making the *volta stabile* simultaneously with the extension of your sword to *gain*. Do not respond in two distinct movements as you will act in two *tempos* and miss the *contro-tempo* moment.

After you have built your comfort with this exercise, you can invite your partner to attack the *high line* or attack your lead leg. The trick to simple decision making here is to always respond by closing the *high line* in *quarta* or *seconda* but be ready to withdraw your lead leg if you realize that it is the target of attack.

Stringere on the Outside, Strike on the Inside

You can follow the steps of the previous exercise but begin on the *outside* and strike on the *inside* instead, as you'll see in these images.

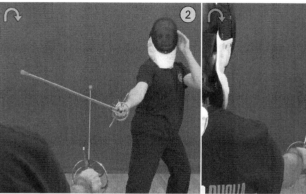

Right has found Left on their outside.　　　Right follows Left's disengage.

Right begins to gain on the inside.

Right gains and strikes in contro tempo in quarta.

Angulation and Penetration

You may have noticed in the previous exercises that the closer you are to your opponent (when you have *found* their sword) the larger the *cavazione* the opponent must make. This is to your benefit. If you can force your opponent to make large movements while you make small movements you'll have a proportional advantage. There are two principles at play that make this happen:

Angulation[38]

In a *finding* position, the steepness of the angle of your sword dictates the amount that your opponent's sword point must drop in order to move from one side to the other.

You can control this angle by reaching your arm and shoulders forward while pushing your hilt downward. Lift your point upward at the same time to make a larger "wall" for your opponent to get around. Note that the tip of your rapier should never go higher than your opponent's head.

Right has a shallow angle. Left can make a small cavazione.

Right has a steep angle. Left must make a larger cavazione.

Creating a steep angle with your sword does not make it any less deadly. A sword does not need to follow the angle of the blade in order to wound successfully with the point. A strike can travel at an alternate angle to the blade, so even though in this extremely angulated position the sword could be said to be pointing over the opponent's head, it is actually threatening the face quite sufficiently. I usually cite to my students during this lesson that swords are not rockets. They are not propelled from their pommels; we can move them along any axis, in any orientation, and the point will strike in just as deadly a fashion. After you have struck, or just before, you can also align the sword more directly at its target.

Creating a vertical distance for your opponent's point to travel is "angulation".

Right strikes Left with their sword at an angle. It will still penetrate.

Right lifts their hilt as they strike to align the blade for greater reach.

Penetration

Angulation on its own is not sufficient to fully control the opponent's weapon; it must be combined with *penetration*. *Penetration* refers to the amount of sword you have crossed, meaning how much of your opponent's sword has passed yours from the place where your two swords intersect. This does not require contact between your swords.

The more of their sword that has passed your own, the more sword your opponent has to move from one side of your sword to the other, thus the longer it takes. If you make a crossing close to the opponent's point, the opponent has very little sword to move from one *line* to another. If there is a larger amount of sword, they'll need to do a lot more work, and they have to get around much more of your sword.

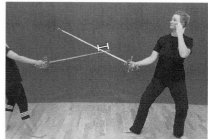 

Right has a small amount of penetration. Left has a small disengage. *Right has a large amount of penetration. Left has a larger disengage.*

You must play a balancing act with *penetration* to *find* as much of the opponent's blade as possible without giving up the *advantage of leverage*.

Experiment with different levels of *angulation* and *penetration* in the previous *contro-tempo* exercises to build a better understanding of how these two important principles make it easier or harder for your opponent to perform a *cavazione* and strike and for you to counter them.

The amount of your opponent's sword that passes your own is the "penetration".

You may notice when you are experimenting with *angulation* and *penetration* that you need to break from the perfect formation of the *guards* you have learned. This is true. The priority is *stringere*. You can safely manipulate the shape of a *guard* provided that doing so restricts targets, invites to an obvious opening, and controls *proportion*.

Right has stringered with a small amount of angulation and penetration, so leans away to create proportion.

The first *terza* on the right creates very little *angulation* and *penetration*, but creates *proportion* by inviting to a target (the head or chest) that is a long way away from the opponent.

The second *terza* on the right creates significantly more *angulation* and *penetration*, prompting a much larger *cavazione*. Even though the fencer's head is closer, the proportional advantage and the ability to gain significantly more *leverage* makes up for it.

Right has stringered on their inside. Their head is close but the angulation and penetration make them safe.

You may feel that your forearm becomes exposed when you push your hilt down and elevate your point. This is true, which is why it is essential that you only create a more extreme angle of your sword once you have crossed your opponent's weapon. In this way you are protecting your forearm with proportion.

When approaching from *out of measure*, be sure to form a *terza* that protects your arm. Only begin to modify your *terza* once you have crossed your opponent's weapon.

Right forms a terza that protects her arm.　　　　*After sufficiently crossing she lowers her hilt.*

Tactical: Contro-tempo vs Primo Tempo

After practicing the *stringere* and *contro-tempo* exercise, you may be left with a fairly logical question: Why would someone who has been *stringered* attempt to strike if they're so easily overcome by their opponent? There are a few reasons:

1. They may not realize or understand the advantage that you have over them. Not everyone who fences with rapiers learns the principles of sword control, no matter how fundamental they may seem to you now.

2. Combat is a fast moving affair and it's easy to not realize the disadvantage of your position. This can lead you to attempt to strike at the wrong time.

3. Your opponent may be attempting to strike you in *primo tempo* but have missed their moment.

We're going to look at this last one now.

Exercise: Primo Tempo vs Contro-tempo

① Start *out of measure* with both of you in *terza*. Your goal is to strike in *contro-tempo*. Your opponent's goal is to strike in *primo tempo*.

② Now you will both freely approach one another. To succeed in your objective, you must succeed in getting to *misura larga* and have found your opponent's sword. From there, you will be ready to strike in *contro-tempo*. Your opponent will succeed in their objective by striking you in *primo tempo* while you step to *misura larga*. (See the earlier section on *primo tempo* for the techniques on doing this successfully with and without a *cavazione*). Your partner must make a sincere attempt to strike in *primo tempo*. If you arrive at *misura larga*, and they choose not to strike, consider it a point against them.

③ The fact that your opponent wants to strike you in *primo tempo* is what will make them vulnerable to *contro-tempo*. If you can successfully step to *misura larga* before they are ready to strike, their attempt to strike in *primo tempo* will give you the opportunity to strike in *contro-tempo*.

④ Periodically switch roles to understand both sides of the exercise.

The opportunity in this exercise is all about being ready at the right *measure*. If your opponent is ready and waiting while you step to *find* them at *misura larga*, they can strike you in *primo tempo*. If you manage to get to *misura larga* while they're not ready, and they attempt to strike late, then you are ready, and you can strike them in *contro-tempo*.

Right is stepping while Left is ready. Thus Left can strike in primo tempo.

Right missed their chance to strike in primo tempo. Left has successfully stringered Right at misura larga.

Mezzo Tempo

By controlling *angulation*, *penetration*, and *measure*, you can substantially increase the length of an opponent's *tempo* to attack, while decreasing the length of your own *tempo* to strike. In this way, you can make it possible to strike your opponent in the middle of a movement (such as a *cavazione*) before they're even able to threaten you with their point. This opportunity is called *mezzo tempo* which means "half tempo" or "middle tempo".

Exercise: Striking in Mezzo Tempo

① Begin *out of measure* with both you and your partner in *terza*.

② Approach your partner, *finding* their sword on your *outside*. Keep approaching until you have arrived at *misura stretta*. Be sure that you have substantial *angulation* and *penetration*.

③ Your partner will now make a *cavazione* under your sword with the intention of *gaining* and striking on the *inside*.

④ As their sword point begins to drop down to get under your *hilt*, extend your sword forward while keeping your *hilt* low. Strike them with a *firm-footed lunge* to their chest or face. In this way you will catch your partner's sword on the *outside* in the middle of their *cavazione*.

It is important that you begin your motion as soon as you perceive your partner's movement. If you wait too long, they will be completing their action, and the opportunity to strike in *mezzo tempo* will have passed.

Mezzo tempo is generally easier to achieve at *misura stretta* where the length of *tempo* you require to strike is quite short. However, the larger the movement of your opponent, the more *tempo* you have in which to strike, and thus the farther away you can be.

Right begins their approach from out of measure.

Right finds at misura stretta.

Right catches Left in the middle of their disengage.

Exercise: Striking in Mezzo Tempo During a Cut

① Begin at *misura larga*, having *found* your partner's sword on the *outside*.

② Your partner will begin to pull their sword backward, away from your weapon, with the intention of making a downward *cut* to your left side. Because we don't cover *cutting* extensively in this book, it may be worth practicing this *cut* action a few times to get a sense of the motion before you respond to it.

③ As your partner begins to withdraw their sword, follow their weapon backward by moving into *quarta* and striking them with a *lunge* to their upper chest.

You can imagine that an invisible string connects your partner's sword to your point. As they begin to withdraw their sword to prepare the *cut*, the action pulls your point into their body, so they are not able to even begin the descent of their *cut* before they are struck.

Note that the *hilt* is held quite high to protect your face so you are protected from your partner's *cut* if they succeed in making it.

Right has stringered Left at misura larga.

Right begins extending their sword as Left pulls their sword back.

Right strikes before Left's cut begins to fall.

Tempi in Summary

The four *tempos* can be easily summarized:

Primo Tempo: Striking while your opponent steps into *measure*.

Left steps to misura larga.   *Right strikes in primo tempo.*

Due-tempi: Striking while your opponent recovers their sword.

Left recovers after they have been parried.   *Right strikes in due-tempi.*

Contro-tempo: Striking while your opponent attacks.

Left attempts to strike on the outside.   *Right strikes in contro-tempo.*

Mezzo tempo: Striking while your opponent moves their point away from you.

Left begins to pull their sword back to cut.   *Right strikes in mezzo tempo.*

Chapter Ten

*It must be kept in mind that all the motions of the sword are
a signal to those who know how to decipher them.*
—Nicoletto Giganti, *Scola overo Teatro,* 1606

STRATEGY

Webster's defines strategy as "the art of devising or employing plans or
stratagems toward a goal." For our purposes, this is a fitting definition.
Our goal in fencing is generally to defeat our opponent while surviving
the engagement. The plan we formulate, that hopefully takes into
account our own strengths and our opponent's weaknesses, is our
strategy.

The fundamental strategy of Italian rapier is to use strategic constraint
(*stringere*), combined with forward pressure, to reduce the opponent's
options and time, forcing them into a predictable error. When they
make that error you strike.

I call this strategic approach the "True Fight".

In this section, you will develop a fundamental understanding of
the True Fight strategy and explore the exercises that will help you
implement it.

Tactical Conditioning

German Field Marshall, Helmuth Karl Bernhard Graf von Moltke, famously said "No plan survives contact with the enemy." This is as true a statement in fencing as it is in war. You may have a plan when you approach your opponent, but so do they. It is a rare encounter where things go perfectly to plan. To be a successful fencer you must be able to adapt a strategy in real-time.

Though you are going to first learn the True Fight as a flow chart of decisions to be made at each *measure*, a necessarily cerebral process, tactics in swordplay cannot be a front-brain operation. Pausing to consider whether to go right or left, while in the *measure* of a sharp weapon, is too slow.

Tactics in fencing is **the implementation of pre-conditioned responses to new threats and opportunities**. You must train the tactical side of the True Fight into your body and into your instinctive responses. This allows your fighting mind to respond to the situation much faster than your conscious brain.

Every exercise that you perform here must first be understood in a theoretical way and then conditioned through repeated drilling, starting slow and gradually accelerating in speed of practice, so that they become automatic responses in your body.

The True Fight

Combat can be a chaotic environment with the potential for a sword to come from nearly any direction, and left unchecked, an opponent can act in seemingly unpredictable ways. The "True Fight"[39] is an approach to the fundamental strategy of Italian fencing, designed to control the unpredictability of fencing and give you a straightforward and limited selection of options to choose from at each stage of a fight. In this strategy, you will use the mechanical and strategic principles you have learned so far to protect yourself from an opponent's most direct attacks, safely approach your own offensive *measure*, and strike when the opportunity presents itself.

The Rules of the True Fight

1. *Stringere* your opponent at all times.
2. Move forward when you have control to increase advantage or strike.
3. When you do not have control, move backward and recover control.
4. Seek opportunities to strike in one of the *four tempos*.

Success in the True Fight

To succeed at the True Fight, remember to take into account that you are facing a sharp weapon that requires very little force to do you great harm. This should temper your actions in two ways:

1. You must approach with great caution, seeking to control the weapon of the opponent at all times and recover control with wise movement should you lose it.
2. As the distance narrows, safety comes with decisiveness, and valour will be the better part of caution. When the opportunity presents itself, you must strike in earnest and without hesitation.

Remember that your primary objective in a sword fight is to survive. Though self-evident, this overarching objective can be easy to lose sight of in our non-lethal modern world. If you want to truly understand and master the traditional art, you must keep this thought first and foremost in your mind as you practice.

Directions of Movement

When you have control, the fundamental thing you are responding to from your opponent is their direction of movement. Movement is categorized into three basic types:

Forward

Forward movements from the opponent bring them closer to you, such as when they *advance* or attack.

Backward

Backward movements take your opponent away from you, such as a recovery from a *lunge* or a *retreating step*.

Stationary/Fixing

Your opponent might stay still when they're waiting to see what you do next or because they're moving only their sword and not their feet. "Fixing" is a stationary moment when an opponent fails to act (thus they are unprepared to react). This can occur for a myriad of reasons including simply forgetting, being overly tense, or being unready to move.

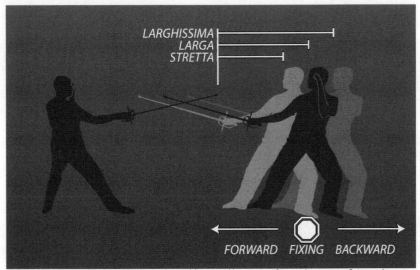

Left has found Right at misura larga. Right could respond by moving forward to stretta, fixing at larga, or moving backward to larghissima.

Circular Footwork

Historical swordplay is by no means restricted to linear action. Many opponents will choose to move right or left in order to gain advantage or find new opportunities. If your opponent is circling, you can still categorize their movement as above. If their circling brings them closer to you, they're moving "forward". If their circling brings them further away, they're moving "backward". If they circle in a manner that keeps them the same distance from you, then they are "stationary."

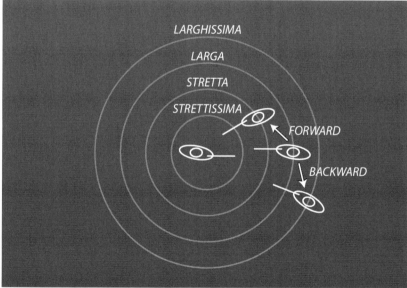

Right could circle forward to stretta or circle backward to larghissima.

Understanding the Flow Chart

The flow chart that follows describes the opportunities that exist at each *measure* to control and strike, not the specific techniques required to do so. It is based on you being the fighter who is in control (has *stringered* their opponent). To stay on the chart you must maintain control as you respond to your opponent's cues. If you lose control you need to recover control to get back on to the chart at a given measure (rule 3 of the True Fight).

Over the next few pages we'll look at how to better understand the flow chart and how to map the correct technique to fulfill each box, maintain control, increase advantage, and strike.

Generally at each stage of the flow chart you will either follow your opponent as they move back (pursue them), acquire more control by stepping to a closer *measure* when they are stationary, or strike them when they move forward (until you're at *misura stretta* where you can hit them regardless of which direction they move).

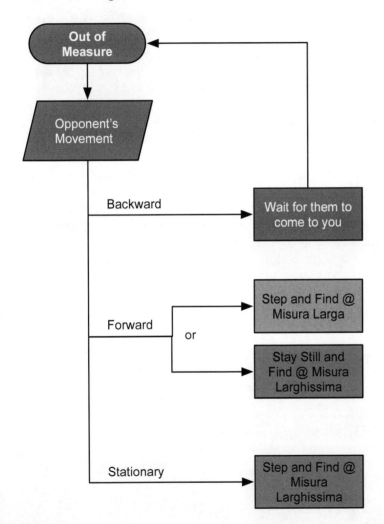

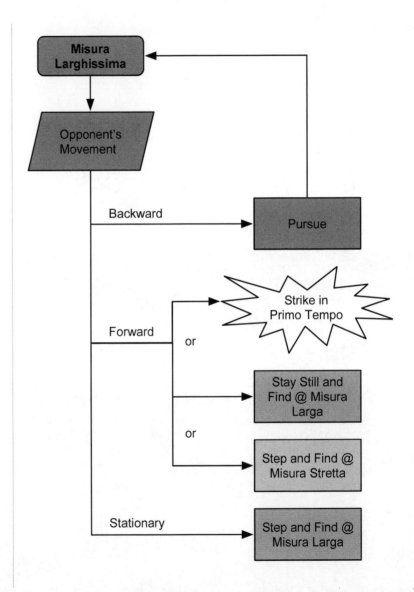

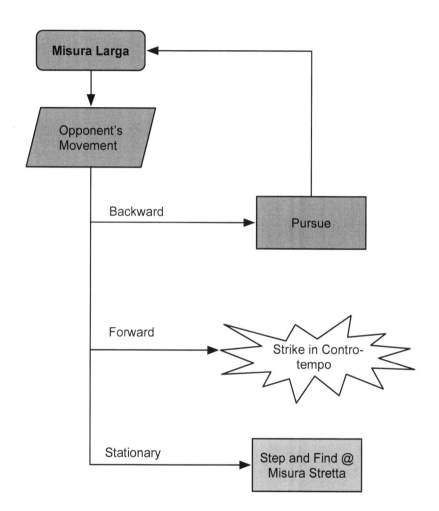

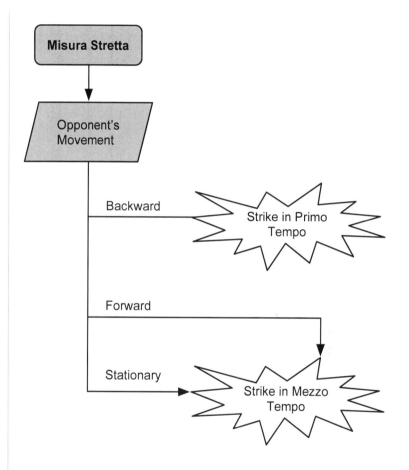

Moving Between Measures

As we explored earlier, the various *measures* are all essentially one step apart (with variance for your own stature and that of your opponent). Movement between *measures* on the flow chart is determined both by your movement and that of your opponent. If your opponent is stationary you can advance between each *measure* one step at a time, through forward movement. However, if your opponent is moving backward while you move forward, your *measure* will not change (unless you take larger steps). Conversely, if both you and your opponent step forward at the same time, you may skip over one *measure* and find yourself two *measures* closer.

Here we will look at how you might arrive at a given *measure* based on the movement choices of you and your opponent.

Arriving at Misura Larghissima

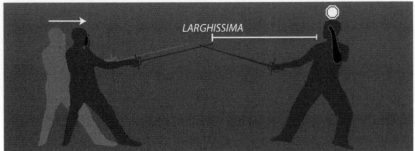

Starting just out of measure. Left steps forward to find the sword of Right while Right fixes.

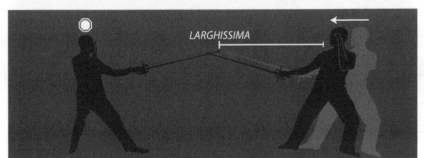

Starting just out of measure. Left waits and finds the sword of Right as Right steps forward to misura larghissima.

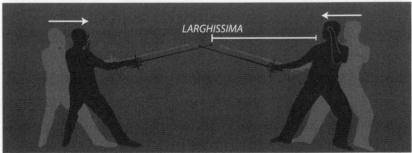

Starting further out of measure. Left steps forward at the same time that Right steps forward. They arrive together at misura larghissima.

Arriving at Misura Larga

Arriving at Misura Stretta

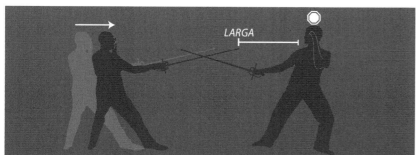

Starting at larghissima. Left steps forward and maintains control while Right fixes.

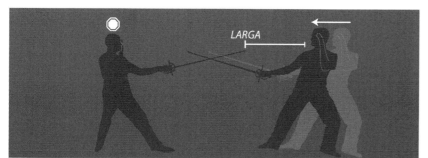

Starting at larghissima. Left waits and maintains control of the sword of Right as Right steps from larghissima to larga.

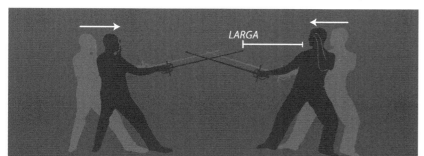

Starting just out of measure. Left steps forward and finds the sword of Right at the same time that Right steps forward. They arrive together at misura larga.

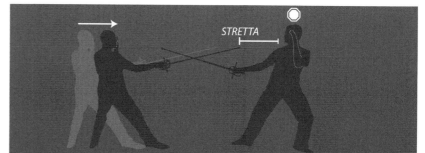

Starting at larga. Left steps forward and maintains control while Right fixes.

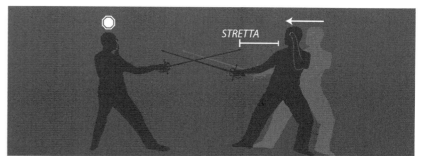

Starting at larga. Left waits and maintains control as Right steps from larga to stretta.

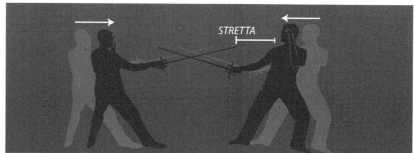

Starting at larghissima. Left steps forward and maintains control at the same time that Right steps forward. They arrive at misura stretta together.

Exercise: Walking the True Fight

In this exercise we are going to fully explore the core techniques of the True Fight. I recommend that you walk through each *measure* with a partner, ensuring you're familiar with the choices and responses that are available to you.

First we will go through the entire flow chart at each *measure* with a focus only on the opponent's direction of movement. Your partner will not change *lines* or attempt to recover control with their sword.

Ideally the exercise will become something you can do from memory.

Misura Larghissima

Practice the three methods for *finding* your partner's sword at *misura larghissima* (on either the *inside* or *outside*):

① Begin *out of measure*. You step forward to *larghissima* and *find* your partner's sword while they stay still.

② Begin *out of measure*. Your partner steps forward to *larghissima* and lets you *find* their sword while staying still.

③ You both begin two steps outside of *misura larghissima* and step simultaneously into *measure*. You *find* their sword while doing so.

If an opponent steps into your *misura larghissima*, with a particularly large step or is particularly unprepared, there is an opportunity to strike them in *primo tempo* with a *passing lunge*.

Having *found* your partner's sword at *larghissima*, have your partner cue you with each movement option, one at a time, resetting to *larghissima* after each cue and response:

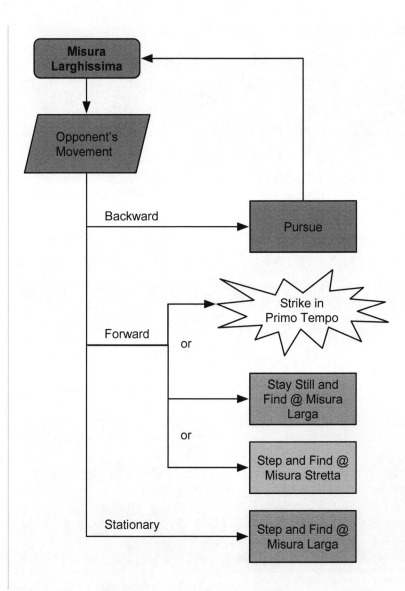

Having *found* your partner's sword at *misura larghissima*, have your partner cue you with each movement option, one at a time, resetting to *larghissima* after each cue and response (in the figures you are represented by the fencer on the right):

① **Cue:** Partner steps away.
   Response: Follow them to maintain *larghissima* and keep advantage over their sword.

② **Cue:** Partner fixes.
   Response: Step forward to *misura larga* keeping advantage.

③ **Cue:** Partner steps forward with a small step.
   Response: Stay still and keep advantage. You have now *found* their sword at *misura larga*.
   OR step forward in the same *tempo* as their step and *find* their sword at *misura stretta*.

④ **Cue:** Partner steps forward with a large step.
   Response: *Gain* and strike in *primo tempo* with a *lunge*.

Left fixes - Find misura larga

Left steps forward - Find stretta

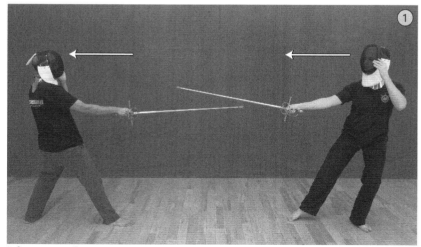

Left steps away - Pursue

Left takes big step forward - Strike in primo tempo

Misura Larga

Practice the three methods for *finding* your partner's sword at *misura larga* (on either the *inside* or *outside*):

① Begin at *misura larghissima*. Step forward and *find* your partner's sword while they stay still.

② Begin at *misura larghissima*. Your partner steps forward to *larga* and lets you *find* their sword while staying still.

③ You both begin *out of measure* (one step outside of *misura larghissima*) and step simultaneously into *misura larga*. You *find* their sword while doing so.

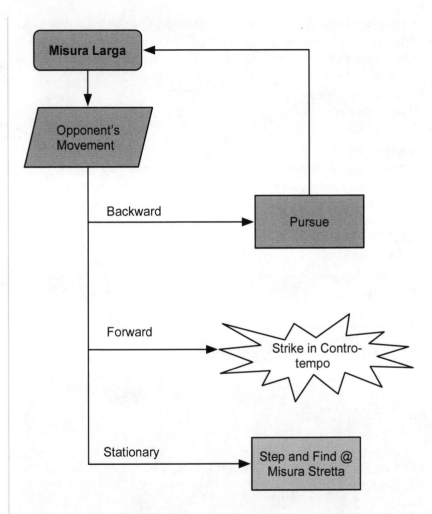

Having *found* your partner's sword at *misura larga*, have your partner cue you with each movement option, one at a time, resetting to *larga* after each cue and response (in the figures you are represented by the fencer on the right):

① **Cue:** Partner steps away.
Response: Follow them to maintain *larga* and keep advantage over their sword.

② **Cue:** Partner fixes.
Response: Step forward to *misura stretta* keeping advantage.

③ **Cue:** Partner steps forward OR attempts to strike with a lunge (without line change).
Response: *Gain* and strike with a *firm-footed lunge* in *contro-tempo*.

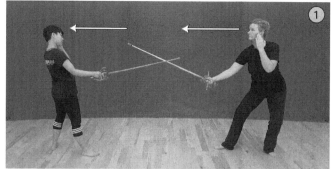

Left steps away - Pursue.

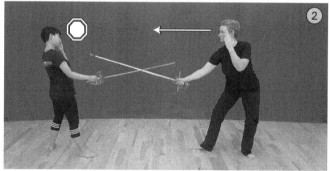

Left fixes - Find misura stretta.

Left moves forward - Strike in contro-tempo.

Misura Stretta

Practice the three methods for *finding* your partner's sword at *misura stretta* (on either the *inside* or *outside*):

① Begin at *misura larga*. Step forward and find your partner's sword while they stay still.

② Begin at *misura larga*. Your partner steps forward to *stretta* and lets you *find* their sword while staying still.

③ You both begin at *misura larghissima* and step simultaneously into *misura stretta*. You maintain *finding* of their sword while doing so.

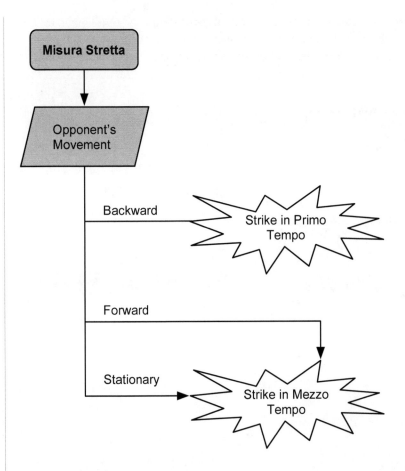

Having *found* your partner's sword at *misura stretta*, you will begin to extend your sword (before your partner even begins to move). Have your partner then respond to this movement with one of the three movement cues. You will adapt to that cue to strike appropriately. Repeat for each cue and response (in the figures you are represented by the figure on the right):

① **Cue:** Partner steps away.
  Response: *Gain* and strike with a *lunge* as they step back to *misura larga* in *primo tempo*.

② **Cue:** Partner fixes.
  Response: *Gain* and strike with a *firm-footed lunge* in *mezzo tempo*.

③ **Cue:** Partner steps forward OR attempts to strike with a *firm-footed lunge* (without *line* change).
  Response: *Gain* them part way through their action, beneath your sword, in *mezzo tempo*.

The last action of *misura stretta* where you strike your partner as they move forward is the only action you will practice at *misura strettissima* in this exercise. The other most common occurrence of *misura stretissima* is after you've *parried* a committed attack.

Left steps away - Strike with a lunge.

Left fixes - Strike firm-footed.

Left moves forward - Strike with the sword low.

Incorporating Line Change

Now we will go through the Walking the True Fight exercise again practicing the techniques required if the opponent changes *line*. Be sure to practice this exercise from a *finding* on both the *inside* and *outside*.

Follow your opponent's movements to maintain control while following the flow chart.

Misura Larghissima

① **Cue:** Partner steps away while making a *cavazione*.
Response: Follow them to maintain *misura larghissima* while making a *contra-cavazione* to maintain control.

② **Cue:** Partner fixes while making a *cavazione*.
Response: Make a *contra-cavazione* while stepping forward to *find misura larga*.

③ **Cue:** Partner steps forward with a small step while making a *cavazione*.
Response: Make a *contra-cavazione* and stay still to *find* their sword at *misura larga* OR make a *contra-cavazione* and step forward to *find* their sword at *misura stretta*.

④ **Cue:** Partner steps forward with a large step while making a *cavazione*.
Response: Make a *contra-cavazione* to *gain* their sword and strike them with a *lunge* in *primo tempo*.

Right has stepped forward making a cavazione. Left makes a contro-cavazione and strikes in primo tempo.

Misura Larga

① **Cue:** Partner steps away while making a *cavazione*.
Response: Follow them to maintain *misura larga* while making a *volta stabile* to maintain control.

② **Cue:** Partner fixes while making a *cavazione*.
Response: Make a *volta stabile* while stepping forward to *find misura stretta*.

③ **Cue:** Partner steps forward, OR attempts to *gain* and strike, with a *cavazione*.
Response: Make a *volta stabile* while extending to *gain* their sword and strike them with a *firm-footed lunge* in *contro-tempo*.

Misura Stretta

① **Cue:** Partner steps away while making a *cavazione*.
Response: Make a *volta stabile* while extending to *gain* their sword and strike with a *lunge* in *primo tempo*.

② **Cue:** Partner fixes while making a *cavazione*.
Response: Make a *volta stabile* and trap your partner's sword beneath your own, part way through their action, striking them in *mezzo tempo*.

③ **Cue:** Partner steps forward, OR attempts to *gain* and strike, with a *cavazione*.
Response: Make a *volta stabile* and trap your partner's sword beneath your own, to strike them in *mezzo tempo*.

Left has disengaged to strike. Right makes a volta stabile and strikes in contro-tempo.

Left has attempted to disengage while staying in place. Right has caught them in mezzo tempo.

Incorporating Pressure

Sometimes an opponent will attempt to recover control while leaving their sword in the same *line* by using a *volta stabile* or simply trying to extend and *gain* your sword (even when you've *found* them already). Even though this option sometimes seems foolish, it is important to practice against it so that you are prepared for an opponent who either doesn't know better or believes that you are not capable of shutting them down.

Walk through the responses at each measure following this guidance:

At *misura larghissima* respond to pressure into the sword by making a *cavazione* and proceeding based on the flow chart.

At *misura larga* if the opponent is applying pressure while moving forward or fixing, you can simply *gain* in response to the pressure, or keep your *finding*. Your advantage should be strong enough that they cannot win the crossing. If the opponent is applying pressure while moving backward, respond with a *cavazione* as you would at *misura larghissima*.

At *misura stretta* you should be able to *gain* in an extended *terza* below your sword, in nearly all cases. If the opponent is moving away, you may need to extend into *seconda* or *quarta* to keep control and maximize your measure but again you should not need to yield to their pressure.

Left is pushing on the sword of Right.   Right can maintain their position or gain.

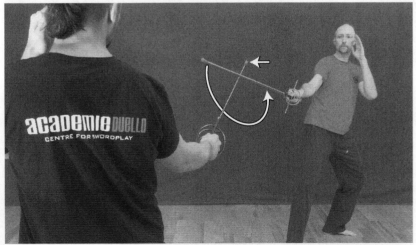

At larghissima. Left pushes on Right's sword with a volta stabile. Right responds with a cavazione.

Recovering Control in the True Fight

In many ways the ideal of Italian fencing is to *stringere* your opponent at the outset and never lose control or have need to back up. However, the reality is that it is hard to keep to this ideal and for many fencing in a more receptive manner, where you allow your opponent some freedom to attack, can be more comfortable and often tactically advantageous.

With this in mind I'd like to take a few moments to review the defensive concepts from earlier in the book and fit them into rule 3 of the *True Fight*: "When you do not have control, move backward and recover control."

Use Distance

The most formidable defensive tool is to stay out of the *measure* of your opponent's attacks. If you find yourself in *measure* without control, simply step away.

If the opponent is attacking, and you have the ability to move (meaning they've attacked *out of tempo*), you can negate many attacks simply by stepping back.

Use the Mirror Movement drill, from the Measure section, and the Gaining Game, from the Recovering Control section, to help you develop a strong sense of your defensive *measure*.

Regain Stringere When It's Lost

If you are in *measure* and have lost *stringere*, move backward and use the techniques from the section on recovering control. Put yourself back into a position of *stringere* over your opponent, then move back in, following the rules of the True Fight. For example, if you step back and have recovered control at *misura larghissima* immediately respond to your opponent's body and sword movement as described on the flow chart.

The figures on the right show three ways that Right can recover control.

Cavazione Sotto: *Right can go under the sword.*

Cavazione Sopra: *Right can go over the sword.*

Volta Stabile: *Right can regain leverage and then crossing.*

Parrying

Parrying is simply *finding* while going backward. When your opponent attacks from a position of control, step backward and *find* their sword. If this is successful, you can begin your responses on the flow chart as soon as you have *found,* even if your opponent is currently in a *lunge.*

Refer to the Defence and Counter-Offence section and the *parata-risposta* exercise from the section on *due-tempi* to see how to use this technique defensively and counter-offensively.

Right has parried the sword of Left by finding it.   *Right has parried the sword of Left by finding it.*

Yielding

At closer *measures* you may find that your only option is to yield and make a *stramazonne*. As advised earlier, it is usually the best practice to cut back to the opponent's weapon to find it while stepping *off-line*. Be aware that you may need to start responding to your opponent's movement and sword action while your sword is still descending to cover their *line*. Follow the rules of the flow chart based on your new measure to respond properly.

Left is yielding in response to the attack of Right.

Chapter Eleven

To one who would become a perfect player, it does not suffice only to take lessons from the master, but it is necessary that he seek daily to play with diverse players, and being able to do so, he must always practice with those who know more than he, because the player with such practiced wits will become most perfect in this virtue.

—Ridolfo Capoferro, *Gran Simulacro dell'Arte e dell'uso di Schermire*, 1610

FROM DRILL TO COMBAT

Crossing blades in a friendly, yet competitive, environment is the true destination for the practice of swordplay. I recommend that once you get the essential motor skills under your belt you begin applying them in tactical exercises and light sparring as soon as possible. Nothing will put technique into context better, or faster, than experience.

This section will guide you on the most productive ways to take what you have learned in this book and apply them in a free and effective manner.

Freeplay

Freeplay is the act of sparring without exercise constraints. It is here that you truly test what you know, learn how you need to improve, and enjoy application of the art.

Different groups govern their freeplay in different ways. At Academie Duello, our open sparring works in this way:

1. Fencers agree to a bout at freeplay.
2. They establish their conventions.
3. They establish their speed.
4. They stand across from one another, well *out of measure*.
5. Salute, and begin fencing based on the established standards.
6. Freeplay continues until someone has been struck in a valid manner.
7. The struck party calls "Hit!" and their opposite says "Thank you" to acknowledge the strike.

Freeplay can then recommence at the salute and continue until both fencers are satisfied.

At Academie Duello, we tend to fence casual bouts in sets of 10. Our focus is on fencing excellence and the ideal of not being struck at all. We try to avoid a misplaced overemphasis on striking. It's easy to forget the tenets and just seek out points. It's important to remember that to strike and not be struck, is the desired outcome. If you strike but are hit as well in a sharp-sword encounter you may not live to know you had "scored".

Sparring at Academie Duello's open sparring night.

General Rules

In all fighting:

- Fence with precision, care, and control at all times.
- Wear appropriate protective gear for the level of sparring you are doing.
- Establish a speed and a convention before fighting.
- Never spar while angry.
- Do not fence faster than your ability to do it well.
- No slapping, punching, kicking, or kneeing.
- No grasping of the opponent's blade.[40]

"Hold"

At a call of "Hold," all fighting stops. "Hold" may be called by either fighter, or an observer, if anything appears to be going wrong, be it gear related (missing gorget, blunt coming off, etc). or psychological (fighter panicking, getting angry, etc).

Valid Blows

A thrust to any valid target. Delivered with the point with sufficient force to be felt. Remember it takes, at most, 6 pounds of pressure to pass through clothing and skin.

A cut to any valid target. We didn't focus on *cutting* in this book at all, but should you begin to incorporate it later, we accept any strike with the edge that meets and passes through its target (the edge slides along and frees on the opposite side) or that makes a substantial movement of the edge, with pressure, along the target (at least 5 inches of travel). The *cut* must first have made at least a 90-degrees preparation (wind-up) so that it would strike with sufficient intention to *cut*, if the blade were sharp.

Conventions

There are two basic conventions we use which establish the valid targets in the bout:

Limited: Only the torso, throat, head, and groin are valid targets. This encourages fencers to go for vital targets and not over-focus on striking hands and arms.

Standard: The whole body is a valid target for a decisive blow.

Scaling Speed

One of the best and most enjoyable ways to step into freeplay is by starting slow and increasing your speed as your competence grows. This type of scaling approach to freeplay will help you build precision, perception, and sensitivity (the feeling of your sword against the opponent's), instead of having all of your hard-earned skills fall apart when you push them too far, too fast.

Our speed levels are:

1. Speed 1
   - As slow as you can go.
   - Each technique can be practiced and thought about as it is executed.
2. Speed 2
   - Deliberately slow.
   - A flowing speed that allows for thought and high mental presence.
3. Speed 3
   - "Walking speed" - neither slow nor fast.
   - Physical forces come into effect. Situations are more fluid and tactical but combat is noticeably slower.
4. Speed 4
   - Fast - smooth and controlled at your perfect form.
   - Physical forces are in play. This is the lower end of "combat" speed.
5. Speed 5
   - Unlimited.
   - There is no restriction on upper speed while still avoiding sloppiness.

Speeds specify upper limit, not uniformity. For example fighting at speed 4 does not require you move constantly at 4, just that you limit your fastest movement to 4.

When working at speeds 1 to 4 be sure to calibrate with your partner to establish agreement. Calibrate to the side of the slower partner.

The Anatomy of a Fight

A fight is more complex than simply approaching your opponent, getting control of their sword, and striking them while they stand there dumbfounded.

There are 5 primary stages to a rapier fight:

1. Assess
   From *out of measure* you assess what you know about your opponent, their physical attributes, combative demeanor (aggressive, passive, forward motivated, patient, etc) and the tactical choices they've made based on their starting *guard*.
2. Engage
   Based on what you determined from your assessment, you must begin seeking control before you arrive to *measure*. You can't simply walk in to the place that you want to strike, you must first engage the opponent's *line* and sword and get them to give you the opportunity to move into *measure* safely.
3. Control
   Once you've bridged past the farthest *measures* you must seek to *find* and maintain control of your opponent's weapon until they give you a safe opportunity to strike.
4. Strike
   From a patient approach and diligent control comes the opportunity to strike with *cover*.
5. Exit Safely
   Having struck your opponent you must still exit from *measure* without giving them any opportunities for a dying strike. You must also acknowledge that sometimes when you strike you miss or fail to sufficiently wound, for these reasons it is imperative that you keep managing your safety until you have fully exited from *measure* after your attack.

Now let's dig into these ideas more fully.

Assess Your Opponent

The True Fight is not uniformly applied. Physical and mental qualities of your opponent will dictate their more likely responses on the flow chart. To formulate how you are going to apply the True Fight be observant from the moment you set eyes on your adversary and throughout each stage of your bout.

Consider the following:

- Height, leg and arm length, and sword length. Is their *measure* likely to be greater, equal, or lesser than yours?
- Posture and chosen *guard*. Are they presenting their sword in a particular *guard*? Are they protecting targets by leaning away or placing their sword in front of them? Which targets seem more exposed?
- Precision and skill. Do they over-move their sword or are they still and precise? Do they take really big aggressive steps or small and thoughtful ones?
- Combative attitude. Are they aggressive or conservative? Forward motivated or waiting for you to come to them?

Adapting to Physical Differences

Taking note of the physical differences between you and your opponent is essential to the techniques you will employ. If your opponent is taller than you, recognize that they are going to be trying to strike you in *primo tempo* earlier than you. It's going to take you more movements to get from *out of measure* into *misura larga* or *stretta*. This will mean that the engagement and control stages of the fight will last longer before an opportunity arises to strike.

Technically you may need to employ more *transports* and you may need to lure them to come to you before you can go to them. See the sections on dealing with the high sword as well as how to defend while stepping forward in the sections on Approaching Different Guards and Defence and Counter-Offence.

If you are taller than your opponent, you'll want to really take advantage of the fact that your *misura larga* may be your opponent's *misura larghissima*. Work to keep them at distance and look for the *primo tempo* opportunities of the True Fight.

If your opponent is stronger than you, you may need to get to a closer *measure* so you can have better *findings* to counteract their strength. If they're really pushy, be prepared to be softer and make more *disengages* and quick sword movements until you find that strong position. Definitely avoid a pushing match. If you're the stronger partner then you can most likely resist your opponent's attempts to *refind* or *parry* your sword in the same *line*.

Responding to Combat Attitude

The more than you can understand someone's tactical approach to their fighting the more easily you can predict which choices they're likely to make. This allows you to reduce the potential responses from your opponent and thus will make you faster to react on the flow chart.

Being a responsive and effective fighter requires that you use good technique to physically reduce your opponent's options (*stringere*) while using good assessment to predict which of the remaining options your opponent is most likely to choose.

Receive an Aggressive Opponent

Opponents who are eager to come forward and rush to the attack can be very intimidating, they can also be some of the easiest opponent's to deal with because they're willing to give you lots of moments to retake control and strike them during errors.

Some general advice:

- Let them come to you. Try to find ways to allow your aggressive opponent to give you control and throw themselves on to your sword.

- Be very aware of *primo tempo* opportunities. If your opponent is coming forward, especially if they're doing it quickly, they're more likely to step heedlessly into *measure*.

- Get to and stay at *misura larga* or *larghissima*. Keeping a little bit more distance between you and your opponent will give you more time to react to a likely attack. Look for opportunities to strike them in *contro-tempo* or *due-tempi* when they attack.

Approach a Conservative Opponent

A more timid or thoughtful opponent may be less willing to approach or attack. They may want you to come to them or may want to see a really good opportunity before they're prepared to take a risk.

Some general advice:

- If they are slow to retreat, move strongly forward to find *misura stretta*.

- If they run away, approach slowly and then back away to encourage them to pursue you. If you can get them moving forward there are opportunities to strike them in *primo tempo* or to step from *misura larghissima* to *misura stretta*.

- Be patient and work to get and stay close. You will need to limit their options with strong *finding* and make it difficult for them to *parry* or escape.

- Give them control so they feel confident to attack or move forward. Then recover control and make a *risposta* in *due-tempi* or pursue them until you are at *misura stretta* and can strike in *primo tempo* or *mezzo tempo*.

A Comment on Receiving, Approaching and Measure

Each *measure* has a speed and an attitude. Generally, as you get closer to your opponent you must act more efficiently and decisively.

Misura larga is a responsive *measure*. Here you lie in wait and force your opponent to give you the opportunity. Because of the space between you and them there is time to perceive and respond to what they do.

Misura stretta is an initiation *measure*. Upon finding *misura stretta*, you must act before your opponent does and adapt to their responses while in motion. If you wait at this *measure*, even if you have *stringered* your opponent, you may lose your position of strength before you realize it. You must come to this *measure* and immediately act or the moment will be lost.

You'll note that in the True Fight flow chart, all of the actions from *misura stretta* are an attack. When you arrive here, because all options are the same, there's no reason to hesitate.

Engagement and Control

Getting into *measure*, while being in control, against an uncooperative opponent, takes some work and finesse, and a whole new level of practice.

The following drills are going to help you combine techniques and responses to get into measure and take advantage of your opponent's reaction.

Exercise: Approach, Control, Strike

In this exercise you will approach your partner, maintain control, come to *misura larga* and strike.

① Approach your partner from *out of measure* with both of you in *terza*.

② Begin to *find* at *misura larghissima* by crossing the point of your sword over your partner's on their *outside*.
Your partner will respond by making a *cavazione* and attempting to *find* you instead on the *inside*.

③ Make a *contra-cavazione* and continue to step forward. You will arrive at *misura larghissima* having found their sword.

④ Your partner will attempt a second *cavazione* while staying in place. You will make a *contra-cavazione* and step forward to *misura larga* having found their sword on the *outside*.

⑤ Your partner will now make a *cavazione* and attempt to *gain* and strike you on the *inside*.
Respond by *gaining* their sword with a *volta stabile* and striking them in *contro-tempo* on the *inside* in *quarta*.

⑥ Recover and *find* your partner on your *inside* in *terza*. Then exit from *measure* keeping *cover* until you're safely away.

The important thing in this exercise is that you need to respond immediately to your partner's actions to maintain control and gain measure. I recommend starting slow (at speed 1 or 2) and then gradually increase in speed as you perfect your timing and precision. This same exercise, and variations of it, can be conducted starting on the *inside* as well.

Right approaches while maintaining control of Left's sword.

Right finds Left on the outside at misura larga. Left begins a cavazione to strike.

Right makes a volta stabile to gain and strike Left on the inside in contro-tempo.

Exercise: Receive, Control, Strike

Let a more forward motivated opponent come to you.

① Begin *out of measure* from your partner with both of you in *terza*.

② Have your partner approach you. Seek to *find* their sword on the *inside* as they do.

③ Your partner will attempt to make a *cavazione* to your *outside* and step to *misura larghissima*.

④ As your partner begins to *find* your sword and step to *misura larghissima*, in the same tempo, make a *contra-cavazione* and step forward. You should now have found them at *misura larga* on the *inside*.

⑤ Your partner will now make a *cavazione* and attempt to *gain* and strike you on the *outside*.
Respond by *gaining* their sword with a *volta stabile* and striking them in *contro-tempo*.

⑥ Recover and *find* your partner on your *outside* in *terza*. Then exit from *measure* keeping *cover* until you are safely away.

Right finds Left on the inside. Left steps forward making a cavazione to the outside.

Right makes a contra-cavazione and steps forward maintaining inside control.

Left makes a cavazione to strike. Right strikes Left in contro-tempo on the outside.

Control and Strike

Against less aggressive opponents, you will frequently need to maintain control for a few *tempos* before an opportunity presents itself. The following exercises will guide you in how to practice this element of combat.

Exercise: Maintain and Strike at Larga

You can either begin this exercise already having found your partner at *misura larga* on your *inside* or you can begin with one of the engagement exercises, described before, to arrive at *misura larga*.

① Your partner will step back while making a *cavazione* to attempt to *find* you on your *outside*.

② You will maintain control by following them and making a *volta stabile* to *find* them on the *outside* instead.

③ Your partner will step back again, making a *cavazione* to attempt to *find* you on your *inside*.

④ You will maintain control by following them and making a *volta stabile* to *find* them on the *inside* instead.

⑤ Your partner will now make a *cavazione* and attempt to *gain* and strike you on the *outside*. Respond by *gaining* their sword with a *volta stabile* and striking them in *contro-tempo* on the *outside* in *seconda*.

⑥ Recover and *find* your partner on your *outside* in *terza*. Then exit from *measure* keeping *cover* until you are safely away.

You can make this exercise more challenging by inviting your partner to step back a random number of times before attempting to strike. They might step back three times and then strike, then only one time. In this way you are training yourself to identify opportunity based on direction of movement.

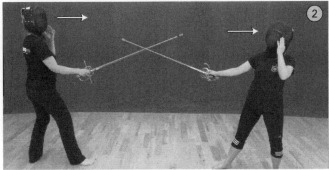

Left has stringered Right. Right steps back and Left pursues, maintaining control.

Right attempts to make a cavazione to gain and strike.

The cavazione is countered with a volta stabile in contro-tempo.

Exercise: Maintain and Strike at Stretta

If your opponent is reluctant to attack, you might need to close to a narrower *measure* to make it difficult for them to avoid being struck. As with the previous exercise, this exercise begins at *misura larga*. You can start this exercise by inviting your partner to find you at *misura larghissima* and then, as they do so, step forward and *find* them at *misura larga* (see the beginning of the Receive, Control, Strike exercise).

① From *misura larga*, your partner will step back while making a *cavazione* to attempt to *find* you on your *outside*.

② You will maintain control by following them and making a *volta stabile* to *find* them on the *outside* instead. Make your step slightly larger, so you get slightly closer as you follow them.

③ Repeat this process of following and taking slightly larger steps until you arrive at *misura stretta*.

④ Having arrived at *misura stretta* immediately begin to *gain* your partner's sword and attack with a *lunge* or *passing lunge*. Trap your partner's sword in the same *line* or follow it into the new *line* (as described in the section on the True Fight). Even when they are being struck, your partner should be backing up and attempting to recover control. The *passing lunge* might be necessary if your partner is taking particularly large or fast steps.

⑤ Recover and *find* your partner's sword. Then exit from *measure* keeping *cover* until you are safely away.

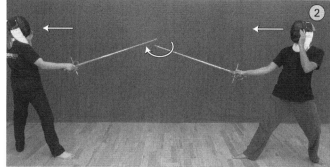

Left steps back and makes a cavazione. Right pursues while maintaining control.

Left steps back again. Right maintains control with larger steps to find misura stretta.

Right initiates their attack at misura stretta and strikes as Left retreats.

Control and Choice

Now we're going to look at how to add choice to drills to make them more tactical.

Exercise: Responding to Direction at Larghissima

① Begin *out of measure* from your partner. Both of you in *terza*.

② *Find* on the *inside* or *outside*, and step forward to *misura larghissima*.

③ Once you have arrived at *larghissima* your partner will do one of three things, which will prompt one of three responses:

  A. Make a *cavazione* and step forward - You will respond by making a *contra-cavazione* to gain and strike your partner in *primo tempo*.

  B. Make a *cavazione* and step backward - You will respond by making a *contra-cavazione* while pursuing them to stay at *misura larghissima*.

  C. Make a *cavazione* and stay in place - You will respond by making a *contra-cavazione* and stepping forward to *misura larga*.

④ You can now reset the drill or if you are at *misura larga* you could integrate the next exercise.

⑤ If your partner was struck: Recover, *find* their sword, and exit from *measure*.

Exercise: Responding to Pressure at Larghissima

① Begin *out of measure* from your partner. Both of you in *terza*. *Find* your partner's sword, on the *inside* or *outside*, and step forward to *misura larghissima*.

② Once you have arrived at *larghissima* your partner will do one of three things, which will prompt one of three responses:

  A. Make a *cavazione* and step forward - You will respond by making a *contra-cavazione* to gain and strike your partner in *primo tempo*.

  B. Make a *volta stabile* and push into your sword while stepping forward - You will respond by making a *cavazione* to gain in the opposite *line* and strike in *primo tempo*.

  C. Step forward while leaving their sword in place - You will respond by *gaining* and striking in *primo tempo* in your current *line*.

③ Recover, *find* your partner's sword, and exit from *measure*.

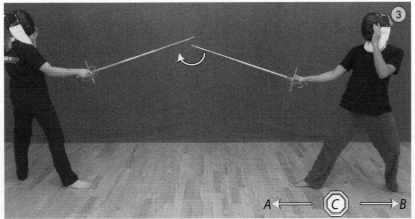

Left has found Right at misura larghissima. Right can step forward (A), backward (B), or fix in place (C).

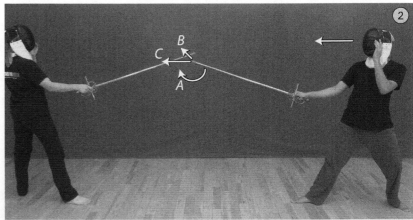

Right can step forward making a cavazione (A), volta stabile (B), or leaving their sword in its current line (C).

Exercise: Responding to Direction at Larga

① Begin *out of measure* from your partner. Both of you in *terza*.

② *Invite* your partner to *find* your sword on your *inside* or *outside*.

③ Your partner will step forward and attempt to *find* your sword at *misura larghissima*. As they do so, make a *cavazione* and step forward, *finding* your partner's sword at *misura larga*.

④ Once you have arrived at *larga* your partner will do one of three things, which will prompt one of three responses:

    A. Make a *cavazione* to attempt to *gain* and strike - You will respond by making a *volta stabile* to *gain* and strike your partner in *contro-tempo*.

    B. Make a *cavazione* and step backward - You will respond by making a *volta stabile* to maintain your *finding* while pursuing them.

    C. Make a *cavazione* and stay in place - You will respond by making a *volta stabile* and stepping forward to *misura stretta*.

⑤ You can now reset the drill or if your partner is at *misura larga* you can immediately repeat the cue and response. If you are at *misura stretta* you could integrate the options of the True Fight flow chart for misura stretta.

⑥ If your partner was struck: Recover, *find* their sword, and exit from *measure*.

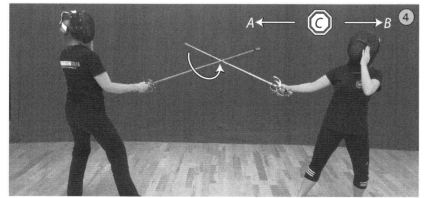

Right can make a cavazione while stepping forward (A), backward (B), or staying in place (C).

Exercise: Responding to Pressure at Larga

① Begin *out of measure* from your partner. Both of you in *terza*.

② *Invite* your partner to *find* your sword on your *inside* or *outside*.

③ Your partner will step forward and attempt to *find* your sword at *misura larghissima*. As they do so, make a *cavazione* and step forward, *finding* your partner's sword at *misura larga*.

④ Once you have arrived at *larga* your partner will do one of three things, which will prompt one of three responses:

    A. Make a *cavazione* to attempt to *gain* and strike - You will respond by making a *volta stabile* to *gain* and strike your partner in *contro-tempo*.

    B. Make a *volta stabile* and push into your sword while stepping forward - You will respond by moving immediately to *gain* their sword in the same *line* to strike in *primo tempo*. If you have *found* your partner properly at *misura larga* you can respond to their pressure simply by *gaining* and maximizing your *advantages*.

    C. Step forward while leaving their sword in place, no pressure applied - You will respond by *gaining* and striking in *primo tempo* in your current *line*.

⑤ Recover, *find* your partner's sword, and exit from *measure*.

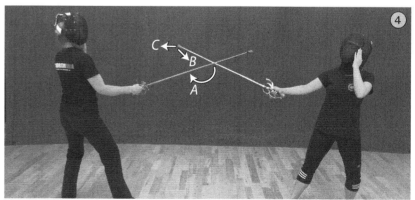

Right can make a cavazione (A), volta stabile (B), or leave their sword in its current line (C).

Making Your Own Tactical Exercises

The previous exercises can serve as a guideline for creating your own tactical exercises. The True Fight flow chart can serve as the basis for the options within the drill and you can incorporate variations of *guard*, changes of control, and anything else presented earlier in the book or that comes up in your freeplay.

Building Difficulty

Start with simple drills (for example with only one option) and seek to have precision and smoothness. Once you are able to perform the technique 80% of the time, begin to add difficulty in two ways:

1. Speed.
   Use the free sparring speeds as a guideline for your drilling practice. Gradually increase the speed to put a skill under pressure. Bring the speed down when it breaks down, fix it, and then push it up again.

2. Complexity
   Add more elements to a drill to make it more like combat and put pressure on your technical ability. As before, if your precision starts to fail, slow it down or reduce the complexity until you're able to stabilize your technique.

Adding Complexity

1. Add Depth.
   Instead of starting *in measure*, make getting to *measure* part of the exercise. In this way, you combine two techniques together and arrive *in measure* in a manner that is more similar to combat.

2. Add Choice.
   Instead of only two options, add in a third or a fourth. The opponent may perform a *cavazione* to strike or simply step backward, forcing you to pursue. You can add options at multiple stages as well, for example: Two options for getting to *misura larga* and then two options to respond to at *misura larga*, based on the opponent's reaction. In this way you will learn how to string several drills together into a more cohesive whole.

3. Add Timing.
   Have your partner change the rhythm of your exercise. When you *find* their sword, sometimes they will respond immediately, sometimes they'll hesitate before responding. This type of variable rhythm is very true to combat and quite challenging to follow without practice.

Tactical exercises allow you to focus on a subset of skills in a way that open freeplay does not. This allows you to more easily diagnose problems and build foundational skills more quickly because they get more direct attention. Learning the art of the rapier is much like learning to play a musical instrument. You start slowly and focus on a small number of skills. As you build proficiency you can add greater complexity and speed. Be patient and intelligent with your practice. Those who allow themselves to go slow learn quick.

The Learning Cycle

The process of bringing a skill from drill into combat is a long one. It takes time, and many hours of purposeful and diligent practice. The more that you understand the process of how a skill is learned and integrated into your art the better you will become not just at fencing but at the process of learning itself.

This chart represents the path of a skill's progression.

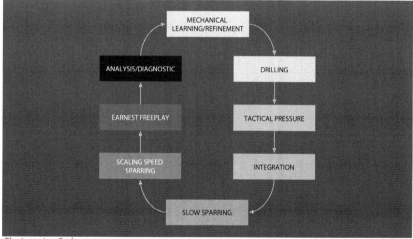

The Learning Cycle

Mechanical Learning/Refinment

First you learn a new skill in isolation with a cooperative partner. You build an understanding of its shape, learn to coordinate it in your body, and achieve its basic goals.

Drilling

Once you can do a technique correctly you repeat that skill over and over to condition your strength and flexibility and to mentally prepare the skill for fast and precise execution.

Tactical Pressure

By increasing the difficulty of your practice through speed and complexity you make application of the skill gradually more true to combat, while allowing you to still focus on doing it precisely.

Integration

Using tactical drills and games (as presented at the ends of most of the earlier chapters) you can create an environment that is more complex than a drill but still presents fewer options than freeplay.

Slow Sparring

Practicing at speeds 1 to 3 is a powerful way to create the environment of freeplay while still allowing you to think, focus on body mechanics, and not get overwhelmed and thus sloppy. Slow sparring plays a significant role in training at Academie Duello and has successfully produced hundreds of top quality rapier fencers.

Scaling Speed Sparring

Deliberately starting slow and then speeding up, then slowing down if things get sloppy, then speeding up again, is a way to challenge yourself to perform faster without jumping off the deep end. There is little value to going full speed but losing all form and mental preparedness. Scaling speed fencing allows you to challenge your edges and gradually increase your mental and physical presence at higher speeds. Again, like playing an instrument, you do not learn to play the piano quickly by smashing the keys as fast as you can. You start slow and gradually build up speed while maintaining precision and tempo at each speed.

Earnest Freeplay

Sword fighting at speed 5 is fun and informative. Use this time to test your skills and learn more about the physical forces that come into play at full speed as well as what is required mentally, and in your body, to respond.

Always use appropriate protective gear and be aware that no amount of protective gear can prevent injury without control and respect for your partner and yourself.

Analysis/Diagnostics

At each stage of this journey there are opportunities to analyze and diagnose your mechanical and tactical challenges. Cultivate the power of critical observation and take what you learn right back to the beginning. Then after you make those fixes mechanically don't just jump right back into full speed sparring and expect a change. The most effective way to make a correction is to bring it back through the process stage by stage from mechanics, through drilling and tactical pressure, integration, and then through the stages of sparring.

The more that you practice this process the better you will get at acquiring and applying new skills. Remember: To learn quick, practice slow.

CONCLUSION

Congratulations on making it to the end of this manual. I hope that your practice thus far has inspired a passion for this art and a desire to take it further. Though this is a manual for beginners, the core of the art is contained herein. I recommend that you read and refer to the book often. Practice every exercise again and make them a core part of your training. As you see challenges in your own freeplay, revisit the exercises that are most pertinent to further refine your ability and place the exercise in greater context.

Though a book is a great way to build a theoretical understanding of a movement art, in the end you need to see it in motion to understand it. My Introduction to Rapier DVD and further lessons presented online at https://www.duello.tv both support and build on the material that was presented here. I recommend looking there to build a better, more dynamic understanding of the exercises and freeplay in general.

I have two subsequent volumes already in the works that will extend your understanding of the rapier and build from the base learned here. These books will teach you two additional strategic approaches: the Deceptive and Adaptive fights. They will also cover the use of secondary weapons such as the dagger, buckler, and cloak, as well as conveying a deeper understanding of rapier play for the intermediate and advanced practitioner.

Beyond these resources, taking physical classes and getting hands-on feedback and the opportunity to spar with experienced practitioners is necessary to solid long-term learning. I recommend that you find a local Academie Duello study group, sister school, or come and visit us in Vancouver. We have ongoing classes, intensive programs, and workshops that occur year-round. We also have distance education programs for those interested in forming their own Academie Duello study group or chapter. Check out the calendar on our website and feel free to be in touch at www.academieduello.com and devon@learnswordplay.com

Enjoy your continued learning, and I hope that we get a chance to cross blades someday in the future.

Devon Boorman

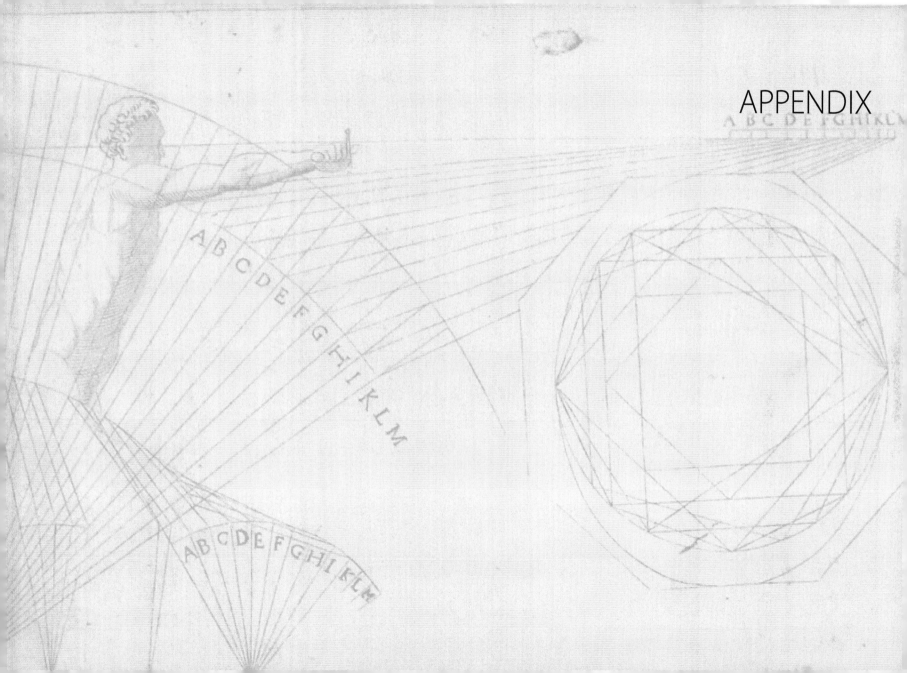

Notes on Historical Terms

As I commented on in the opening chapter of this book, my goal as a teacher is to convey an authentic form of swordplay grounded in physics, tactics, and mechanics. I seek to do this in the most effective and direct manner possible, while honouring the original sources for these arts. To that end, I have used terminology from several sources and have applied stricter meanings to many terms to add clarity and aid learning. In many cases I have also added new terms that I felt best highlighted important points in the learning process. However, if you intend to work with original sources, which I hope you do, you may find it helpful to understand some of the decisions that I have made and how terms and approaches may differ in the manuals of the original masters. To that end, I have used endnotes throughout the book and included additional notes and information in the glossary. For those things that were not best covered in those two places I am including a few additional notes:

Regarding the Guards

Though presented in this book in an exact way, each *guard* can have many different forms both in my system as well as across historical systems. A single source may show several different formations of a single named *guard* with the primary commonality being the hand position. Salvator Fabris in his section on the sword alone describes 2 different formations of *prima*, 6 of *seconda*, 3 of *terza*, and 9 of *quarta*.

Ridolfo Capoferro describes *terza* in one manner in the first section of his manual, and then shows as many as four variations of how the body might be held. The hand orientations are also not explicitly described, simply the hand's relation to other parts of the body (which are also not consistently described).

Camillo Agrippa, the originator of the four hand positions, shows a set of four arm and body positions but says that many different variations can be formed from them.

When working with historical sources, be sure to thoroughly read the descriptions of desired body postures as presented by that particular author and do not come with any preconceived ideas.

Finding, Gaining, and Constraining

The biggest difference in terminology in my approach from some historical sources is that I have given distinct meanings to the words: *find* (trovare), *gain* (guadagnare), and *constrain* (stringere). Historically these terms are used interchangeably and the concepts that I represent quite distinctly are themselves treated in a more holistic sense. I have found that there is a significant pedagogical benefit to dividing the degrees of mechanical control from one another (*finding* and *gaining*), and dividing the mechanical from the strategic (*finding* vs *stringere*). By giving strict codifications to these concepts students gain a new and finer power over them. It does mean however that when working from a related historical source that you need to use the context of the words, to a greater degree, to understand that author's specific meaning.

The Four Tempos

The opportunities to strike an opponent become more clearly defined as you move into fencing works in the 1500s. The manuals of Antonio Manciolino (1531), Achille Marozzo (1536), and Giovanni dall'Agocchie (1572) describe, at various points, opportunities to strike after the weapon has passed, in the preparation of an attack, after you have set it aside, and while the opponent steps toward you. The codification of specific named *tempos* (*primo*, *contro*, *due*, *mezzo*) then becomes more clear in 17th century fencing manuals where the authors were strongly influenced by Aristotle's ideas on time and motion.

Each author has slightly different definitions for each of the *tempos* but they are largely in-line with what I present here. As you move past the rapier period into the 18th and 19th century some of these same terms persist but often with quite different connotations.

Glossary

These are the terms that are used in this manual and in my system of teaching. Where there are significant differences, I have included a reference to the historical uses of these same terms.

Advancing Step

A small step toward the opponent performed by moving the front foot first, followed by the back foot.

Battere / Battuta (To Beat / Beat)

To strike your opponent's blade with your own to send it *off-line*. This is typically done to create an opening or draw a predictable response from your opponent.

Closed Line, Close the Line

A *line of attack* that cannot be followed because a weapon or other defensive object has gotten in its way. *Lines* are commonly *closed* through *gaining*, where the *three advantages* are fully acquired and applied against an opponent's sword.

Cavazione (Disengage)

To move your point from one side of your opponent's sword to the other, with the intention of moving into a position of advantage or away from a position of disadvantage. This is generally done by moving the point in a V or U shape over or underneath the opponent's blade.

Cavazione in Tempo (Disengage in Time)

A *cavazione* performed at the same time that your opponent seeks to *find* your sword. You typically follow this with an immediate attack.

Cavazione Sopra (Disengage Over)

A *cavazione* where your point moves from one side of the opponent's blade to the other by drawing an upside down V over its point.

Closed Position

Taking a *guard* with the *off-hand* placed immediately beside the sword arm, behind the *hilt* of your rapier. In a *closed position* the available targets are *outside* the sword and outside the *off-hand*.

Cone of Protection

The cone-shaped deflection created by your *hilt* and *forte* by having them extended in front of your body. Similar to the effect of creating a large shadow with a small object by placing it closer to the light source.

Contra-Cavazione (Counter Disengage)

A *cavazione* performed in response to your opponent's *cavazione*, in the same *tempo*. This *cavazione* is typically done to return you to your original *line*.

Contro-tempo (Counter-time)

To strike in the *tempo* of your opponent's attack.

Counter-Attack

An attack made in *contro-tempo* or in *due-tempi* immediately following a displacement of the opponent's blade.

Cut

An attack delivered with the edge of the rapier.

Constrained Line

A *line of attack* that is not *closed* but has been compromised because the opposing sword fighter has *found* it by applying a greater portion of each of the *three advantages*.

Crossing

See *Three Advantages*.

Debole (Weak)

The upper half of the sword's blade used primarily for wounding with it's point or edge. Also the part of a sword that is most easily moved around by the opponent (the farthest place on the lever arm).

Defensive Posture

A position of the body and sword where the sword is positioned in front of the flank. The shoulders and head are reclined away from the opponent.

Due-tempi (Double Time)

To strike your opponent in a *tempo* where they are recovering their sword. This is done in two *tempos*. For example in the first *tempo* you *beat* your opponent's sword, sending it *off-line*, in the second *tempo* you strike your opponent as they attempt to bring it back *on-line*.

False Edge

The edge opposite the *true edge*. When the sword is held in *terza* with the point elevated, this edge faces the wielder.

Filo Dritto (True Edge)

See *True Edge*.

Filo Falso (False Edge)

See *False Edge*.

Find, Finding

See *Trovare la Spada*.

Firm-Footed Lunge

An attack made without moving the feet. This is done by extending your upper body and pushing your hips forward onto your front foot.

In historical sources the term *pie fermo* (fixed-footed in English) can refer to an attack where neither foot moves, or where the back foot stays in place and only the front foot moves (see *lunge*).

Four Tempos

The four categories of opportunities to strike. For more see *Tempo*.

Freeplay

A form of sparring without any exercise constraints. The goal being to get as close to a simulation of real combat as possible while maintaining control and ensuring the safety of you and your partner.

Forte (Strong)

The lower half of the sword's blade used primarily for defence. Also the part of your sword best for applying pressure to your opponent's weapon (the part of your lever closest to the fulcrum).

Fuori Misura (Out of Measure)

To be far enough away from your opponent that you cannot strike them, and they cannot strike you, in a single motion. This is at least one step outside of your opponent's *misura larghissima*.

Gain, Gaining

See *Guadagnare*.

Guadagnare (To Gain / To Earn)

To fully acquire the *three advantages* over the opponent's sword and thus close their direct *line of attack* while also forcing your *line of attack* to stay *open*.

This term appears in most Renaissance fencing treatises but is generally used interchangeably with *stringere* or *trovare la spada* and its full, nuanced, meaning needs to be derived from its context.

Guardia (Guard)

An optimal position of sword and body with the primary purpose of defence. A good guard:

• Minimizes targets.

• Presents threat to the opponent.

• Creates powerful alignment for fencing actions.

• Creates strategic and tactical advantage.

Guards are a combination of one of two body and arm postures: *defensive* and *offensive*; and one of four hand orientations: *prima, seconda, terza,* and *quarta*.

Each of the four *guards* carries a default body position, unless otherwise stated. For example, *prima* is paired, by default, with the *offensive posture*. A request to form *"prima guardia"* refers to the specific hand orientation and default body posture.

High Line

A *line of attack* above the opponent's sword hilt.

Hilt

The protective portion of the sword that includes and surrounds the handle. This includes the handle, *sweepings, rings, knuckle-bow,* and *quillons*.

The *hilt* is sometimes called the "guard" of the sword.

See the rapier diagram on page 16 for more detail.

Inside Line

If you hold your sword in your right hand, the *inside line* is a *line of attack* to the left of your sword. Note that when referring to *lines of attack* it is important to reference the subject and the *line*, for example: The opponent's *inside line*.

In-Tempo

To move at the same time as your opponent, with movements that are equal or lesser in length. See *Tempo*.

Invitation

The *opening* of a *line of attack* for your opponent, with the intention of getting them to attack along it. This is generally done as part of a plan that will lead you into a position of greater strength or to an opportunity to strike.

Knuckle-bow

A bow shaped piece of metal in the *hilt* that protects the hand and fingers on the *true edge* side of the rapier.

See the rapier diagram on page 16 for more detail.

Leverage

See *Three Advantages*.

Line

The term *line* could refer to a *line of attack* (for example, "the *inside* or *outside line*") or the *line of direction* (for example, "place your feet on the *line*.")

Line of Attack

The path that a sword travels along to strike your opponent.

Line of Direction

An imaginary straight line, running along the floor, between you and your opponent. When forming a *guard* you stand with both feet on this line.

Low Line

A *line of attack* below the opponent's sword hilt.

Lunge

A movement, made typically with an attack, where the combatant takes a large step with their front foot, while propelling themselves by straightening their back leg.

Measure

See *Misura*.

Measure, In

To be within one of the five measures and thus able to successful reach your opponent with an appropriate attack based on that *measure*. See *Misura*.

Measure, Out of

See *Fuori Misura*.

Mezzo Tempo (Half Time / Middle Time)

The opportunity to strike an opponent half way through an action. Typically this is to strike the opponent while they prepare to attack, or in the beginning of an attack before the threat has developed. If you strike them in the final part of the attacking motion you are striking in *contro-tempo*.

At the beginning stages of a student's fencing education, I use *mezzo tempo* quite strictly to mean: a short attack that occurs while the opponent prepares to attack (i.e. withdraws their sword for a cut) or while the opponent makes a non-attacking motion at a close *measure*. However, *mezzo tempo* can refer to a strike that lands in the beginning of an attacking movement. For example, striking someone in the arm as they begin a *thrust* or just as a cut begins to fall. This usage is also more common in historical sources.

Misura (Measure)

The distance you must cover in order to strike your opponent. Measured from the point of your sword to your opponent's body. There are five measures: *Fuori misura* (out of measure), *misura larghissima* (widest measure), *misura larga* (wide measure), *misura stretta* (narrow measure), and *misura strettissima* (narrowest measure).

Misura Larga (Wide Measure)

The distance at which you can strike your opponent to the body with a *lunge*.

Misura Larghissima (Widest Measure)

The distance where you can strike your opponent with a *passing lunge* to the body or a stepping *lunge* to the arm.

This term is not used in historical sources from the rapier period.

Misura Stretta (Narrow Measure)

The distance at which you can strike your opponent to the body with a *firm-footed lunge*, where both feet stay planted and the hips shift forward over the lead leg.

Renaissance authors describe *misura stretta* based on the placement of the feet as well as the distance of the point to the target. Capo Ferro describes two definitions, one based on being able to reach the opponent with no movement of the feet, the other based on a small increase of the foot (perhaps where the sword is already extended, so less movement is required than if you were in a *defensive posture*).

Misura Strettissima (Narrowest Measure)

The distance at which you can strike your opponent simply by moving from the *defensive posture* to the *offensive posture*. I.e., simply with an extension of the sword, arm, and shoulders.

Capoferro describes *misura strettissima* as the distance where you can strike the opponent in the uncovered sword or dagger arm without a step.

Offensive Posture

A position of the body and sword where the sword is extended in front of the lead shoulder with the chest and shoulders forward and the hips held over the rear foot. This position is often a transition position between the *defensive posture* and an attack.

Off-hand

The hand you are not holding your sword in.

Off-line

To have your point directed away from your opponent. This typically occurs as a result of an error or because your point has been sent *off-line* by your opponent through an action such as a *beat*.

Off-Side, Off-Hand Side

The side of your body associated with your *off-hand*. If you are holding your sword in your right hand, this would be your left side.

On-line

To have your point directed at a target. The opposite of *off-line*, where the point is not directed at a target.

Open Line

A *line of attack* that leads directly to your target and has no influences applied over it by your opponent (the *line* has not been *found* or *gained*). As you travel this *line*, you may acquire one, or all, of the *three advantages* over the opponent's sword.

Open Position

Taking a *guard* with the *off-hand* placed to the outside of the face. When in an *open position* the available *lines* for the opponent are *outside* the sword and between the sword and *off-hand*.

Out of Tempo

To move while the opponent is stationary and *in measure*. The risk is that the opponent can respond to your movement to gain advantage or strike.

Outside Line

If you hold your sword in your right hand, the *outside line* is a *line of attack* to the right of your sword. Note that when referring to *lines of attack* it is important to reference the subject and the *line*, for example: The opponent's *outside line*.

Parata (Parry)

A defensive *finding* done in response to an attack. This is done by acquiring the *three advantages* over that attack while keeping the *hilt* low and the point high, or the *hilt* high and the point low.

In sources on Renaissance rapier, a *parata* may refer to an exclusively defensive action or to an action that also contains an immediate or simultaneous counter-attack. In this terminology, *gaining* someone's sword, in response to an attack, could be referred to as "parrying". In this book, a "parry" refers specifically to *finding* the sword in a purely defensive capacity.

Parata-Risposta (Parry-Response)

A *parry* that is followed in the next *tempo* by an attack. This attack is typically performed in *due-tempi* in response to the recovering of the opponent's sword from the *parry*.

Parry

See *Parata*.

Passata (Passing Step)

A step made towards or away from your opponent by crossing the lead leg behind the rear, or crossing the rear ahead of the lead. The orientation of the feet and hips is maintained throughout this step.

Passing Lunge

An attack made by passing the rear leg ahead of the lead leg. The orientation of the feet can be maintained, or the body can be rotated to bring the *off-hand side* ahead of the *sword-side*.

Prima (First Hand Position), Prima Guardia (First Guard)

An orientation of the sword hand and arm that turns the knuckles toward the ceiling. As a *guard* it is formed in the *offensive posture* with the sword positioned above the *sword-side* shoulder, with the point straight toward the opponent.

Primo Tempo (First Time)

To strike your opponent in a single *tempo* while they perform a non-offensive action. Some examples include: As your opponent steps into your *misura larga*, when at *misura larga* your opponent moves their sword non-offensively, or when the opponent fixes in place long enough for you to strike.

Proportion

The comparison of the size of your movements (*tempos*) to those of your opponent. It is generally good practice to make movements that are smaller or equal in size to those of your opponent. In this way you are more able to respond to your opponent *in-tempo* and not be struck in *primo tempo*, *due-tempi*, *contro-tempo*, or *mezzo tempo*.

Making your actions smaller than those of your opponent is one of the first well-documented ideas of using *tempo* to your advantage. Antonio Manciolino describes striking in *mezzo tempo* by using mezzo colpi (half blows) in contrast to colpi finito (full blows).[41]

Quarta (Fourth Hand Position), Quarta Guarda (Fourth Guard)

An orientation of the sword hand and arm with the knuckles towards the *inside line* (the left, if you are right handed). As a *guard* it is formed in the *offensive posture* with the sword positioned in front of the *off-side* shoulder, with the blade, and point, directed straight toward the opponent.

Quillons (Crossbar)

The bars that protrude from one or both sides of the *hilt*, in alignment with the *true* and *false edge*, used to control the opponent's sword and make a *cavazione* more difficult for them to perform.

See the rapier diagram on page 16 for more detail.

Rapier

A primarily civilian sword typical of the 16th and 17th centuries with a long blade and complex *hilt*. For a full description of its anatomy and associated terms see the rapier diagram on page 16.

Retreating Step

A *small step* away from the opponent performed by moving the back foot first, followed by the front foot.

Ricasso

The unsharpened, often square edged, part of a sword's blade, just ahead of the *quillons*. On rapiers, this section of the blade is often surrounded by the *rings* and *sweepings* and is thus within the *hilt*.

Rings

The circular bars that protect the hand as part of the *hilt*.

See the rapier diagram on page 16 for more detail.

Seconda (Second Hand Position), Seconda Guardia (Second Guard)

An orientation of the sword hand and arm with the knuckles towards the *outside line* (the right, if you are right handed). As a *guard* it is formed in the *offensive posture* with the sword positioned in front of the sword-side shoulder, with the blade, and point, directed straight toward the opponent.

Small Step

A step performed by moving one foot forward a half foot-length, so the distance between the feet expands, and then catching up with the opposite foot so the feet return to their original distance. See *advancing* and *retreating step*.

Small steps are not clearly defined in Renaissance fencing texts. In some cases they are not used at all in favour of the *passing step*.[42]

Sparring

A simulation of sword combat within the exercise and practice environment. At Academie Duello it is performed based on a set of conventions and speeds.

Stringere (To Constrain)

Placing your sword in a position of strategic advantage that forces your opponent to move in a way that gives you a *tempo* to act. This is generally done by *finding* their sword.

The technique of *stringere* employs *constraint*, to reduce an opponent's options; *invitation*, to predict the opponent's next action; and seeks to lengthen the *proportion* of the opponent's next action in relation to your own counter to that action. When using *stringere* you control *proportion* through three aspects of the crossing of your sword and your opponent's:

- Breadth — The lateral distance between your opponent's sword and yours that must be travelled for your opponent to change *lines*.
- Angulation — The vertical distance, created through the angle of your sword, that your opponent must travel with their point in order to change *lines*.

- Penetration — The amount of your opponent's sword that has passed your blade. The greater this length, the longer the length of action to change *lines*.

Stringere, as a term, appears in most Renaissance fencing treatises but is generally used interchangeably with *guadagnare* (gaining) or *trovare la spada* (finding) and its full, nuanced, meaning needs to be derived from its context. The terms *breadth*, *angulation*, and *penetration* are used in many different ways across fencing texts from the Renaissance to modern day. This usage is entirely my own pedagogical device, though the principles applied through them are apparent within the historical practice of Italian rapier fencing.

Sweepings

Curved bars that connect the *rings*, *knuckle-bow*, and *quillons* as part of the protective furniture of the *hilt*.

See the rapier diagram on page 16 for more detail.

Sword-hand

The hand you are holding your sword in.

Sword-side

The side of your body of your current *sword-hand*. If your sword is in your right hand, this would be your right side.

Tempo (Time)

Tempo in fencing has several meanings:

- The rhythm in a fight. Like taking turns in a game. The speed and measure of this rhythm is its tempo. If you are moving and pausing at the same time as your opponent you are said to be *in-tempo* with them.
- The measurement of stillness and motion. "A tempo" is a unit of movement bounded by two stillnesses, or a stillness, bounded by two movements. The length of a *tempo* can vary. The comparison of the length of your *tempos* to those of your opponent is called *proportion*.
- A moment of opportunity to strike. *Tempo* in this definition is divided into four types: *primo tempo*, *due-tempi*, *contro-tempo*, and *mezzo tempo*.

Terza (Third Hand Position), Terza Guardia (Third Guard)

An orientation of the sword hand and arm with the knuckles towards the floor. As a *guard* it is formed in the *defensive posture* with the *hilt*, elbow and hand positioned in front of the flank. The point is directed straight at the opponent's flank or upward toward their chest or face.

Terza Guardia is the most defensive of the *guards* and is the usual starting position for a swordplay bout.

Three Advantages

Three aspects of blade relationship that give you mechanical strength over your opponent's weapon. They are:

- True Edge – Turning your *true edge* towards the opponent's blade.
- Crossing – Orienting your blade so that it crosses over the top of your opponent's.
- Leverage – Crossing your opponent's blade in such a way that their *debole* (weak) is closer to your *forte* (strong).

In historical sources these *advantages* are never explicitly codified or collected in this way, however they are applied. *Leverage* is the most explicitly described of the *advantages* and is usually covered through dividing the sword into parts, with as few as two[43] and as many as twelve,[44] and then describing how to connect them. In all Renaissance rapier texts you see the *true edge* used to *close lines of attack*, however the authors seem to expect an existing understanding of this on the part of their readers. *Crossing* is more ambiguously defined; Salvator Fabris states that the sword's *edge* is strongest in the direction the sword points. Ridolfo Capoferro says, that when approaching on the *inside* to point toward the opponent's *sword-side* shoulder and when approaching on the *outside* to point toward their *off-side* shoulder.[45] He also makes specific mention of which eye to strike[46] in particular actions, to further emphasize the crossing of the sword (though this reason is never explicitly mentioned).

Transport

A method of *finding* or *gaining* the sword of the opponent where you move it from its current *line* into another. For example you might *find* your opponent on your *high inside* and then move them using the *advantage of leverage* into the *low outside* as you *gain* them. *Transports* are often used as a means of safely striking targets that are below the sword.

Thrust

An attack delivered with the point of the rapier.

Trovare la Spada (To Find the Sword)

Placing your sword in a position of mechanical advantage over your opponent's sword that *constrains* their *line of attack* and facilitates your ability to gain their sword in that same *line*. *Finding* is done with or without contact and is done by acquiring a greater amount of the *three advantages* than your opponent. *Finding* is generally used to *stringere* the opponent (constrain them strategically).

Historically this term is used primarily by Salvator Fabris to describe both a mechanical and strategic position over the opponent's weapon. His meaning moves between *finding*, *gaining*, and *stringere* (as I use them) based on context.

True Edge

The primary cutting *edge* of the sword. Aligned with the sword's *knuckle-bow* and the knuckles of the wielding hand.

True Fight

A fundamental fencing strategy based on *stringere*, moving forward when in control, backward to recover control, and striking in the four *tempos*.

The True Fight can be summarized into a flow chart that gives set actions at each *misura* based on whether or not an opponent changes *line* with their sword and their direction of movement: forward, stationary, or backward.

See the True Fight in the Strategy chapter.

The "True Fight" is a pedagogical invention of mine that is part of a three part system that includes the Deceptive Fight (a combative approach that involves misleading the opponent) and Adaptive Fight (an approach that involves continual movement forward). In historical Italian fencing texts this term is not used, however the concepts of these three fights are employed by various authors.

Volta Stabile (Stable Turn)

To rotate the *edge* of the sword from one facing to another. For example, to turn its *edge* from the left to the right. Sometimes this facing change is accompanied by a movement of the point to simultaneously acquire the advantages of *crossing* and *leverage* over the opposite *line of attack*.

This term is not used in Renaissance era rapier texts. It has been pulled forward from the Medieval work of Fiore dei Liberi where it has a similar meaning. Within the Bolognese texts they sometimes refer to this movement as a mezza volta of the hand (half turn of the hand).

1 Ben Jonson fought a rapier duel with actor Gabriel Spenser in 1598. Spenser was killed and Jonson was arrested. He narrowly avoided the death penalty. — *Locating the Queen's Men, 1583-1603: Material Practices and Conditions of Playing*; Ostovich, Syme, Griffin; Ashgate publishing; 2009; page 91.

2 The artist and friend to Van Gogh, Paul Gauguin, was an active fencer and potential duelist. In the book *Pact of Silence*, historians Hans Kaufmann and Rita Wildegans make an interesting argument for Van Gogh's famous ear mutilation being the occurrence of a sword encounter between the two artists that was then covered up to protect Gauguin from prosecution. *Pakt des Schweigens*, Osburg Verlag, 2008.

3 Introduced for epee in 1936, foil in 1956, and sabre in 1988. International Fencing Federation history, www.fie.org

4 Though in most Zorro depictions the weapon is a classical sabre, with the notable exception of 1998's *Mask of Zorro* starring Antonio Banderas, where he uses a rapier.

5 There are a few exceptions to this: *Paradoxes of Defence* by George Silver (1599), where Silver identifies and derides the techniques of the "rappir" for their excessive focus on duelling, and champions the use of the backsword as well as other contemporary weapons. Joachim Meyer's *Kunst des Fechten* (1570) also identifies the "rappier" as a weapon brought to Germany from foreign sources and distinguishes its techniques from other weapons such as the messer and two-handed sword.

6 More reading on the military revolution and its affect on the noble classes can be found in "The Military Revolution, 1550-1660" by Michael Roberts. Published in *The Military Revolution Debate: Readings on the Military Transformation of Early Modern Europe;* Boulder, CO; Westview Press; 1995.

7 *Il Libro del Cortegiano*, Aldine Press, 1528, page 25.

8 Most judicial duelling codes go back to the 9th century. In the late 14th century we see the introduction of the Code Duello to specify how honor plays into the judicial duel. Prior to this, duels are of two kinds: judicial duels over property disputes, and trials by combat to settle a "high crime": murder, rape, incest or treason. Technically, heresy is a high crime, but the Church never accepted dueling as a legitimate judicial act, *Ivanhoe* not withstanding. You can read more about this in "The Judicial Duel in 16th Century Italy", Tomasso Leoni, *In the Service of Mars, Volume 1, Proceedings from the Western Martial Arts Workshop 1999-2009*, pages 237-250. Many examples of judicial duelling in armour can be seen in early fighting manuals such as those by Hans Talhoffer (1443 and later)

9 Pietro Monte was an historian and fight master of Spanish or Italian origin who published several books in the early 1500s in Italy. He is favourably mentioned by many contemporaries including Castiglione and Leonardo da Vinci.

10 More on the cultural pressures that lead to the evolution of the duel in Italy can be found in the book *Il Duello Giudizaiaro per Punto D'Onore* by Marco Cavina, Giappichelli, 2003

11 Achille Marozzo's 1536 manual instructs its reader on use of the sword in one-on-one encounters as well as against men on horseback, with diverse armaments, and in judicial duelling.

12 From *Fencing: A Renaissance Treatise by Camillo Agrippa*, a translation of *Trattato di Scientia d'Arme con un Dialogo di Filosofia*, by Ken Mondschein, Italica Press, 2009.

13 This is a calque from the Italian term *spada di lato* - literally translated as "sword of the side". Perhaps more properly translated as a dress sword or sidearm. A weapon that can be easily carried in a civilian context.

14 In the post-mortem inventory of the goods of Duke Alvaro de Zúñiga. The term *epee rapiere* first appears in French writing in 1474. AVB Norman, *The Rapier and Small-Sword* 1460-1820, Ken Trotman Publishing, 2010.

15 Ariel Roth notes the consequence of duelling in France in the early 1600s: "In France during the reign of Henry IV, more than 4,000 French 'gentlemen' lost their lives in an eighteen-year period." *The Dishonor of Dueling*; Roth, A.A.; Grisda.org; 1989.

16 *Gran Simulacro dell'Arte e dell'Uso della Scherma* was first printed in Siena in 1610.

17 Giganti published two books: *Scola, overo teatro* was first printed in Venice in 1606 and *Libro secondo di Niccoletto Giganti* was published in 1608.

18 *Lo Schermo, overo Scienza d'Arme* was first printed in Copenhagen, Denmark, in 1606.

19 *La Scherma di Francesco Fernando Alfieri* was first printed in Padua in 1640.

20 Capoferro comments that all defences should contain an offence and all offences a defence. Earlier manuals such as those by Antonio Manciolino (1523), and Achille Marozzo (1535) emphasize specifically defensive actions ahead of attacks. George Silver, an English Fencing master, in his (1599) manual also derides the Italianate rapier and its emphasis on single time actions, versus the more conservative, and traditional, defence and counter attack methodology of the broadsword and backsword as practiced at the time in England.

21 17th-century rapier manuals from Iberia, the Netherlands, Belgium, and Germany all depict complex hilted swords oriented toward thrusting oriented play.

22 Based on the paper "Some Medicalogical Aspects of Stab Wounds" by Dr. Bernard Knight published in the 1976 *Legal Medicine Annual* where Dr. Knight tested the resistance of human skin to knives. SCA member Chris Zakes attempted a similar test with fencing foils and reproduction rapiers. His studies found that most reproduction rapiers required 4 lbs of pressure to penetrate a soaked raw hide designed to approximate human skin. The test is conducted by placing the point of the weapon against the skins surface and gradually applying pressure until the point penetrates fully through the skin.

This type of measurement provides an easy to comprehend but scientifically imprecise measurement of force. A more extensive breakdown of force requirements for penetration of various types of tissue including skin, muscle, and fat, can be found in "Dynamics of stab wounds: force required for penetration of various cadaveric human tissues" *Forensic Science Volume* 104, Issue 2.

23 A stage actor inadvertently stabbed a colleague to death during a stage performance of *Romeo and Juliet*. The unlucky young man delivered a thrust at the very moment his vision was inadvertently obscured by a member of the cast. Although he claimed to have felt no resistance, a post mortem examination revealed that he had penetrated the chest of the victim to a depth of eighteen centimeters. Thimm; *Supra* volume 6; page 463.

24 For a study of the tactical and performance outcomes of asymmetry and symmetrization in Judo practitioners see: Stanislaw Sterkowicz, Grzegorz Lech, Jan Blecharz "Effects of laterality on the technical/tactical behavior in view of the results of judo fights" *Science of Martial Arts* volume 6, issue 4; 2010.

25 For a study of asymmetry and its impacts on the performance and injuries in Volleyball, a highly asymmetrical sport, see H.K. Wang T. Cochrane "Mobility Impairment, Muscle Imbalance, Muscular Weakness, Scapulary Asymmetry and shoulder injury in Elite Volleyball Players" *Journal of Sports Medicine and Physical Fitness* 2001;41:403-10

26 "Item, her majesty also ordereth and commandeth that no person shall wear any sword, rapier, or suchlike weapon that shall pass the length of one yard and half-a-quarter of the blade at the uttermost, nor any dagger above the length of 12 inches in blade at the most, nor any buckler with any point or pike above two inches in length. And if any cutler or other artifices shall sell, make, or keep in his house any sword, rapier, dagger, buckler, or suchlike contrary thereunto, the same to be imprisoned and to make fine at the Queen's majesty's pleasure, and the weapon to be forfeited; and if any such person shall offend a second time, then the same to be vanished from the place and town of his dwelling." - *Tudor Royal Proclamations* (3 Volumes). Edited by Paul L Hughes and James F Larkin. Yale University Press, New-Haven and London, 1969. (ABNRID 63013965 //r97) volume 2, page 278.

27 "A Comparison of Late 16th to Early 17th Century Rapiers with Modern Reproductions" - DI (FH) Florian Fortner, Julian Schrattenecker, BSc, Fechtschule Klingenspiel, Vienna.

28 Defining these two fundamental positions is my own device. Not all historical Italian masters advocate distinct upper body positions, nor explicitly define them. I have found that learning through this approach helps students best understand how to control their bodies and defend themselves through good sword and body relationships.

29 The terms "open position" and "closed position" are distinct to my practice. You see these postures employed throughout historical Italian texts as well but they are never systematically defined in this way.

30 Originally conceived by Françoise Mézières, a teacher and practitioner of physiotherapy throughout the 20th century, a muscular chain is a group of at least 2 polyarticular muscles (meaning they extend over a minimum of two joints) running in the same direction and overlapping like tiles on a roof without any interruption in the linkage. Where this occurs in the body, all the muscles in the chain are mutually dependent and behave as though they are a single muscle. The longest such chain is the posterior chain which runs from the back of the skull down our spine, backs of our legs, all the way to our toes.

31 The term "finding the sword", or in Italian *trovare la spada*, and "gaining the sword", *guadagnare la spada*, are used subtly differently in my teaching than in historical sources. I have outlined the distinctions in the Appendix.

32 Agrippa's four hand positions represented a significant simplification of the system of fencing. Prior to Agrippa, Italian authors describe as many as 15 to 20 different hand and arm positions.

33 The term *cavazione* (and it's English equivalent: disengage) are used differently in modern fencing than they are in renaissance texts. In many, a cavazione includes a movement to control or strike. I use the term at its barest to mean a movement of the point from one side of the opponent's weapon to the other.

34 I have borrowed this term from Fiore dei Liberi's early 15th-century works. Its usage amongst modern instructors varies. Be aware.

35 In my teaching I de-emphasize the term "parry" as it suggests to many a purely defensive action of the sword. It is essential to recognize that whether you are finding while your opponent is standing still, coming to find you, or coming to strike, the mechanics of the final position, and your follow-up, are essentially the same. The goal is to have a position that protects you from the most direct lines of attack, presents a threat to your opponent, and allows you to proceed forward to strike or gain greater advantage.

36 The term "stramazzone" and "tramazzone" are used in historical Italian fencing works to refer to a wheeling cut that is generally aimed to hit the opponent but can also be used to strike or defend against an attack, as we are doing here.

37 In historical sources the term stringere is used interchangeably with the terms *finding* and *gaining* to mean both mechanical and strategic constraint. I have found it useful in my pedagogy to separate the idea of mechanical control and strategic control.

38 This term is being used here specifically to refer to the angle of your sword. It can sometimes be used to refer to movement of the sword around an opponent's weapon or movements of your feet that take you off the line.

39 The True Fight is a pedagogical approach to understanding fundamental Italian fencing strategy. Though the named concept is one we use exclusively at Academie Duello, the principles of it are applied by the traditional rapier fencing masters. At Academie Duello the True Fight is part of a 3-part strategic system that also includes the Deceptive Fight and the Adaptive Fight. More on these in future volumes.

40 Grasping the blade of the opponent's sword with your off-hand is an advanced technique that can only be executed safely under very specific circumstances. Grasping the sword at this stage of your learning is almost certainly counterproductive to your, and your sparring partner's, learning.

41 An example of this is in the first section of Antonio Manciolino's *Opera Nova* (1531).

42 Salvator Fabris specifies the use of the passing step over the advancing and retreating step in his "book 2". In this book his goal is to move continually, and smoothly, toward the opponent. This is more easily done with the passing step because the advance and retreat necessarily create pauses as you expand and contract the distance between your feet.

43 Ridolfo Capoferro in his *Gran Simulacro* defines the *forte* and *debole* of the sword and admonishes other masters who make further divisions. Ridolfo Capoferro, *Gran Simulacro*, 1606, page 15.

44 Gérard Thibault, a Flemish fencing master, uses precise divisions and relationship instructions ("place your 7 on the opponent's 9") in his 1630 rapier manual *Academie de l'Espée*.

45 In the description of plate 15. — Capoferro, Gran Simulacro, 1606, p.76.

46 An example is plate 7 where he states "D lo ferisce di punta ne l'occhio sinistro di piè fermo". Translation: D makes a firm-footed thrust to their left eye. Ridolfo Capoferro, *Gran Simulacro*, 1606, page 60.